Forestry Commission
Handbook 1

Forest Insects

A guide to insects feeding on trees in Britain

By D. Bevan

Formerly Principal Entomologist, Forestry Commission

The author was greatly helped during the compilation of this handbook by T G Winter, J T Stoakley, M R Jukes and C I Carter

LONDON: HER MAJESTY'S STATIONERY OFFICE

HMSO BOOKS

HMSO publications are available from:

HMSO Publications Centre
(Mail and telephone orders only)
PO Box 276, London, SW8 5DT
Telephone orders 01-622 3316
General enquiries 01-211 5656
(queuing system in operation for both numbers)

HMSO Bookshops
49 High Holborn, London, WC1V 6HB   01-211 5656 (Counter service only)
258 Broad Street, Birmingham, B1 2HE   021-643 3740
Southey House, 33 Wine Street, Bristol, BS1 2BQ   (0272) 24306/24307
9–21 Princess Street, Manchester, M60 8AS   061-834 7201
80 Chichester Street, Belfast, BT1 4JY   (0232) 238451
13a Castle Street, Edinburgh, EH2 3AR   031-225 6333

HMSO's Accredited Agents
(see Yellow Pages)
and through good booksellers

ISBN 0 11 710200 8

ODC 453 : 145·7 : (410)

Keywords:

Insects, Entomology, Forestry

Acknowledgements

Line drawings by N J Fielding
Stereoscan photographs by M R Jukes
Colour photographs from the Forestry Commission collection
The photograph of *Tetropium gabrieli* is by Dr M Speight

Enquiries relating to this publication should be addressed
to the Technical Publications Officer, Forestry Commission Research
Station, Alice Holt Lodge, Wrecclesham, Farnham,
Surrey GU10 4LH

Contents

Introduction

Most students of the author's generation were brought up on Dr Neil Chrystal's *Insects of the British woodlands* published in 1937. Before that foresters had A.T. Gillander's *Forest entomology* (1912), and the excellent papers of Prof. R. Stewart MacDougal, many of them published in the *Transactions of the Royal Scottish Arboricultural Society*, were also notable contributions to early knowledge of forest insects. The great expansion in plantation forestry followed upon the end of the first world war. Many of the earlier crops planted have since reached maturity, been felled and replaced and so it is that the forester has, in a short time, gained a great deal of new knowledge about the particular problems associated with the different phases of crop life. As new habitats have been created, insect species have found conditions propitious for establishment and, in some cases, for great increase.

This work is targeted primarily at the field forester and manager, the arboriculturist, the student, the biology teacher or field naturalist. It is divided into two parts; the aim of Part One is: firstly to provide a quick tool for identification of insects, down to species where possible, or to group where greater precision demands the service of a specialist; secondly to give some idea of the forest importance or ecological significance of the species found.

The choice of species included in Part One is not entirely as idiosyncratic as it may seem at first! Most of the species are common subjects of enquiry whether for the damage they cause or through some eye-catching characteristic of their appearance, behaviour or activity. A few foreign species considered to have a high pest potential have also been included – as much as a reminder that the flow of exotic pests has been a feature of afforestation and is likely to remain so, as it is to provide characters by which the species might be spotted on arrival.

Part Two deals with the more important pest species, or groups of species, and summarises accumulated experience of their patterns of behaviour, site preferences and potential for increase.

The 'way into' the book is outlined on page 6. An experienced user's point of entry will obviously depend as much on the state of his knowledge as it will on whether he finds the larva or the damage.

Recognising and dealing with pest organisms, both insects and fungi, do pose real problems to the generalist or practical man, as they do indeed to the specialist facing specimens outside his range of particular expertise. There are some 22 000 insects recorded in Britain and the late George Gradwell was fond of remarking that oak forest had about half the insect species recorded in Britain associated with it in one way or another. In addition there are many species which cannot be run down to specific level on a single specimen and many which can only be identified by a full time specialist in that particular group.

I have concerned myself here only with those insects that rely on the tree directly for food – the primary trophic level of the ecologist.

Since the forester's concern is with the insect stage which damages, emphasis must be placed in most cases upon the immature insect – with the important exception of the Coleoptera in which Order the adult quite frequently surpasses the larva in both longevity and appetite. The List of Insect Orders (page 8) has been included primarily for quick reference purposes. For those who wish to tackle the identification of adults I would suggest as a next step the key in the Collins *Guide to the insects of Britain and western Europe* by Michael Chinery (1986).

Conventionally larvae are classified into 'types' within a framework of a series of recognisable embryological development phases. There are both marked variations within the 'types' as well as adaptations to specific feeding environments. As a result there are a plethora of shapes, sizes and forms within individual Orders and across a wide range of Orders. For anyone wishing to enter this rather esoteric field *How to know the immature insect* by H.F. Chu (1949), is to be recommended. Meanwhile, we shall have to find our own unsteady way through the field by a less sophisticated means – the Guide to Insect Larvae on page 10 (one developed from an original by Miss J.M. Davies). The guide will certainly be found over-simplified for more refined tastes and a little latitude is recommended in its use.

The references have been chosen in order that the reader can gain easy access to more detailed information than presented here and to provide a first 'entry' into the literature. Wherever possible selection has favoured a late date, English language, and a premium has been put on availability. The four volumes, in German, by Schwenke (which are to be highly recommended as general reference) are here used where no alternative in English could be found.

This handbook should be regarded as one of a family of three Forestry Commission publications on insects. This volume aims to aid recognition and enable the reader to take decisions appropriate to his field. It covers some 280 or so species. A second publication, *A catalogue of phytophagous insects and mites on trees in Great Britain* by T.G. Winter (FC Booklet 53), provides a list of some 1500 species of insects and mites on trees, with insects names and authorities according to revised Kloet and Hincks (published by the Royal Entomological Society of London), up-dated where necessary. It also provides English names and a list of the species under their host plants. The third publication is *The use of chemicals in forest and nursery* (due for revision as a FC Bulletin), which reflects both up-to-date attitudes to the use, as well as choice of, insecticides and other pesticides.

I have to thank all my old colleagues in the Entomology Branch, both at the Northern Research Station and at Alice Holt Lodge, for their help with this publication. They will no doubt be involved in future gathering of further information upon the species covered and upon species yet to demand recognition. It is equally certain that I have failed to recognise some sources of knowledge, both people and literature. I would therefore encourage anyone who feels there have been omissions worthy of future inclusion to please make contact with the Entomology Branch of the Forestry Commission's Research Division.

DERMOT BEVAN

How to use the Handbook

The handbook has been divided into two main parts. In addition there is a list of Insect Orders, a Guide to Insect Larvae, a section of colour photographs and a list of literature references.

List of Insect Orders and Guide to Insect Larvae

Forests team with insects of many Orders and representatives of all those in the LIST OF INSECT ORDERS on page 8 may be found in woodland as well as many species of mites, spiders and other arthropods. All combine and interact to recycie basic materials and nutrients to perpetuate the forest ecosystem. Some breed or feed in or on trees, others depend on herbs, mosses, lichens, fungi, bacteria, yeasts or woody litter. Some are parasites, hyperparasites, superparasites or predators upon others and there are those which acquire their needs from what the others have left behind. Use the GUIDE TO INSECT LARVAE on page 10 or silhouettes in the LIST OF INSECT ORDERS on page 8 to help you distinguish between the tree feeder and the closer of its associates.

Part One: Tree Hosts, Insects and Damage

Insects have been placed under the HOST TREE GENUS upon which they feed (e.g. *Quercus* – oak, or *Larix* – larch). Within the GENUS they have been listed according to the PART OF THE TREE on which they will be found, starting at the top of the tree with LEAF and working down to ROOTS and finally WOOD.

Part Two: Principal Forest Pests

A few species, or groups of species, are dealt with in more detail. A short summary of their more recent history in Britain is given and their significance to the management and conservation of the crops upon which they feed is discussed. All are cross-referenced between the two Parts and the colour section.

Bark beetles are illustrated in a section of black and white stereoscan photographs.

How to use Part One

HAVING   found the INSECT or associated DAMAGE

IDENTIFY   the HOST TREE GENUS

NOTE   the TREE PART upon which the insect is feeding

IF   DAMAGE only is seen – Go direct to Part One

OR   if it is a NYMPH – Go to the silhouettes in the LIST OF INSECT ORDERS p.8

     if it is a LARVA – Go to the GUIDE TO INSECT LARVAE on p.10

THEN GO TO   PART ONE: CONTENTS p.13 and thence to appropriate page for TREE GENUS

THEN   consider alternatives offered for fit, and identify either by:
TREE PART and ORDER OF INSECT married to DAMAGE
or
TREE PART and DAMAGE only

USE   COLOUR SECTION for further identification check if insect is illustrated

FAILED?   you may have found a species which feeds on a number of HOST TREE GENERA

GO TO   either to BROADLEAVES GENERAL, pp.14–19 or CONIFERS GENERAL, pp.58–61.

NOTE   DAMAGE RATING and pick up REFERENCE to literature or to COLOUR PLATES

N.B. The immature insect may be a LARVA, e.g. a maggot, caterpillar, etc., or a NYMPH with a generalised likeness to the adult.

List of Insect Orders

1. *THYSANURA* Bristle-tails (Silver fish) 2. *DIPLURA* Two-pronged Bristle-tails 3. *PROTURA* 4. *COLLEMBOLA* Springtails	Adults wingless Immature stages – small versions of adult		APTERYGOTA (= AMETABOLA)
5. *EPHEMEROPTERA* Mayflies 6. *ODONATA* Dragonflies 7. *PLECOPTERA* Stoneflies 8. *ORTHOPTERA* Grasshoppers and Crickets 9. *PHASMIDA* Stick insects 10. *DICTYOPTERA* Cockroaches 11. *DERMAPTERA* Earwigs 12. *PSOCOPTERA* Booklice 13. *MALLOPHAGA* Biting and Bird lice 14. *ANOPLURA* Sucking lice 15. *THYSANOPTERA* Thrips 16. *HEMIPTERA* Bugs, Aphids, Adelgids, Leaf hoppers, Cicadas and Plant hoppers	Adults winged Immature stage – NYMPH (Usually bears semblance to adult but smaller and wingless)	EXOPTERYGOTA (= HEMIMETABOLA)	PTERYGOTA (= METABOLA)

17. *NEUROPTERA*
Lacewings and Snake flies

18. *MECOPTERA*
Scorpion flies

19. *LEPIDOPTERA*
Butterflies and Moths

20. *TRICHOPTERA*
Caddis flies

21. *DIPTERA*
Flies

22. *SIPHONAPTERA*
Fleas

23. *HYMENOPTERA*
Bees, Wasps, Ants, Sawflies
and Ichneumon flies

24. *COLEOPTERA*
Beetles and Weevils

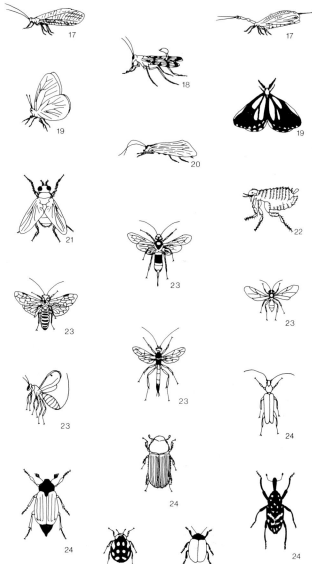

Adults winged
Immature stage – LARVA
(Quite different from
adult form, turning into
a chrysalis or pupa)

ENDOPTERYGOTA (= HOLOMETABOLA)

PTERYGOTA (= METABOLA)

Guide to Insect Larvae

WITHOUT THORACIC LEGS OR PROLEGS (SEE FINAL COLUMNS)

WITH PROLEGS

Mouthparts
well developed.
Head dark.

Body white and
wrinkled.
COLEOPTERA
Scolytidae 1
Curculionidae 2
(Bark beetles and
weevils).

Thin, elongate, white,
brown or pinkish.
Usually 5mm or less.
Under bark.
DIPTERA 3, 4 & 5
(Various midge
families).

Elongate, greyish-white.
5 mm or less.
In organic soils.
DIPTERA
Bibionidae

Less elongate.
Leaf miners.
LEPIDOPTERA 6
DIPTERA

Mouthparts reduced.
Head pale.
Body white and
wrinkled.
HYMENOPTERA
Ichneumonidae 7
Braconidae
and other parasite
families, also bees,
ants, wasps and
gall wasps
(*Cynipidae*)
and seed wasps
(*Chalcidae*). 8

Mouthparts and head
greatly reduced.
Body tapering to front.

Patterned or marked
in green or brown.
Slug-like.
DIPTERA
Syrphidae 9
(Hoverflies).

More elongate.
White, brown or
pinkish larvae
under bark.
DIPTERA 10
(Various midge families).

Often orange, white
or brown.
Usually 5mm or less.
DIPTERA
Cecidomyidae 11
(Gall midges).

5 pairs of prolegs
on segments 3–6
and last.
LEPIDOPTERA 12
(Most butterflies
and moths).

Less than 5, normally
2 pairs of prolegs
on segments 6 and 7.
LEPIDOPTERA
Geometridae 13
(Loopers).

More than 5 pairs of
prolegs on segments
2–7 and last.
HYMENOPTERA
(Sawflies). 14

15

7

9

12

8

11

10

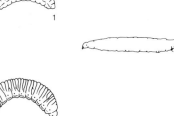

13

14

3

1

17

4

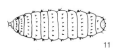

2

5

18

6

WITH THORACIC LEGS

WITHOUT PROLEGS

THORACIC LEGS WELL DEVELOPED

THORACIC LEGS POORLY DEVELOPED,
VESTIGIAL OR MISSING

**BODY WITH
ARMOURED
DORSAL PLATES**

Spindle-shaped.
Mandibles
sickle-shaped.
NEUROPTERA 15
(Lacewings).

Thinner and tapering
to rear.
Mandibles stronger.
Under bark.
MEGALOPTERA 16
(Snakeflies)

More cylindrical.
Mandibles caliper
shaped.
*COLEOPTERA
Carabidae* 17
(Ground beetles).

Body often tapering
to rear but similar
to above.
Mandibles stronger.
*COLEOPTERA
Staphylinidae* 18
(Rove beetles).

Elongate 'polished'
reddish brown.
*COLEOPTERA
Elateridae* 19
(Wireworms)

**BODY SOFT, HEAD
ARMOURED**

BODY STRAIGHT

Elongate, under bark,
COLEOPTERA

white, 5mm.
Nitidulidae 20
(*Rhizophagus*)

Pink, blue/grey
colour, dotted
or striped, 15mm.
Two hooks at rear.
Cleridae 21
(Ant and Chequer
beetles).

BODY CURVED

More oval, with dots,
tubercles and hairs.
COLEOPTERA

Coccinelidae 22
(Ladybirds).

Sometimes with hairs.
Chrysomelidae 23
(Leaf beetles).

Root feeder.
*COLEOPTERA
Scarabaeidae* 24
(Cockchafer).

Similar to above but
in rotting wood.
*COLEOPTERA
Lucanidae* 25
(Stag beetles).

Wood borers.
Less than 10mm
Less curved.
*COLEOPTERA
Anobiidae
Lyctidae* 26
(Furniture and
Powder post beetles).

HEAD DARK

Head sunk into thorax.
Body usually flattened.
*COLEOPTERA
Cerambycidae* 27
(Longhorns).

Very flattened.
Head wide.
Larva club shaped.
*COLEOPTERA
Buprestidae* 28
(Flat-headed borers).

HEAD PALER TO
YELLOW-BROWN

With short terminal
spine.
*HYMENOPTERA
Siricidae* 29
(Wood wasps).

With long armoured,
swordlike terminal
process.
*COLEOPTERA
Lymexelidae* 30
*Hyloecoetus
dermestoides*

Elongate 'polished'
reddish brown.
*COLEOPTERA
Elateridae* 19
(Wireworm).

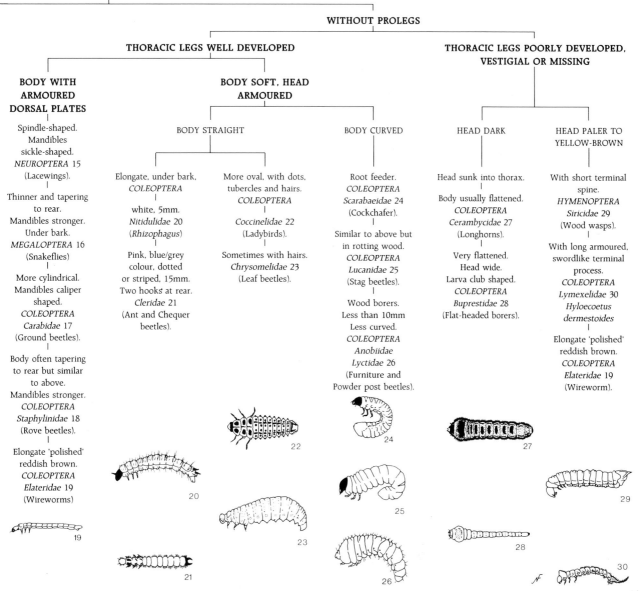

19

20

21

22

23

24

25

26

27

28

29

30

KEY TO DAMAGE RATINGS

XXXXX   Very severe. Causing death of crop.

XXXX   Severe. Causing severe loss of crop increment, death of individual trees, severe degrade of produce, of young stock, or of amenity value.

XXX   Important. Causing significant loss of increment or value.

XX   Less important. Causing some check, loss of increment or value.

X   Not important. Obvious but with slight or no effects on crops or individual plants. (Including insects with pest status established elsewhere but not so far in Britain.)

s   Secondary (e.g. most bark beetles). This category is reserved for pests which attack after some known primary cause. They may none the less be very important.

*   Species deemed to have high plant health risk rating but not known as breeding species in Britain.

Note: The measurement at the end of a description is the length of the damaging stage of that insect; it does not refer to the part of the body which may have been last mentioned in the description.

Part One: Tree Hosts, Insects and Damage

PART OF TREE	DESCRIPTION OF DAMAGE AND FEEDING HABIT	DESCRIPTION OF DAMAGING STAGE *(see note on p.12)*

BROADLEAVES (GENERAL)

LEAF	Feeds as a colony of nymphs upon xylem sap of a number of broadleaved trees, within a large blob of froth. When feeding actively the froth drips. *A. salicina*, a unicolourous, pale brown relation is less common and confined to sallow. Both overwinter as eggs.	Dark brown bug with fawn saddle markings. Head pointed. 8mm.
LEAVES	These seven species are only part of the defoliating complex which commonly attack a wide range of both forest and fruit trees as well as shrubs. There are a number of other species some of which are very difficult to separate in the larval (i.e. the damaging) stage, and by no means easy as adults. The dominance of one species depends on occasion and woody species attacked. *O. brumata* and *E. defoliaria* are commonly of most importance on oaks with *E. autumnata* next in importance. *O. fagata* and *A. aurantiaria* often dominate on birch. The females in *O. brumata*, *O. fagata*, *E. defoliaria* and *A. aurantiaria* are without wings or bear vestiges only.	A paler form is light green with a usually green head. A darker form is blackish-green and has a dark head. The upper of the three side lines is thinner than in *O. fagata* (below). 15–22mm.
		Light green sometimes with grey stripe down back. Three white-yellow lines on each side, upper wider than in *O. brumata* (above). Head and spiracles black. 15–22mm.
		Colour variable. Reddish brown above yellowish on sides and below. Also a black side line edged with interrupted white. Head brown. 25mm.
		Yellow to reddish with brown lines down back. Purplish lines on sides, dark striped yellowish under. Head light brown. 25–36mm.
		Golden green to apple green with a green head. Three light side lines, upper ones thin, lower ones distinct. Spiracles light brown. 20–27mm.
		Very variable. Twig-like with head deeply notched. Either greenish and faintly dotted in white with faint purple central line, or brownish. 40–50mm.
		Twig-like, greyish or greenish-brown, stout, tapering slightly to grey-brown head. Two rows of warts down back. 35–45mm.

TIME OF DAMAGE	STAGE	ORDER AND FAMILY	LATIN NAME	ENGLISH NAME	TYPE OF CROP	DAMAGE RATING *(see key p.12)*	REFER-ENCE
June to mid-Aug.	NYMPH	HEMIPTERA Cercopidae	*Aphrophora alni*	Broadleaf spittle bug	All ages	XX	108 116
May to June Adult Nov./ Dec.	LARVA	LEPIDOPTERA Geometridae	*Operophtera brumata* Plate 51	Winter moth	All ages	XXX	138 141 140
May to June Adult Oct./ Jan.–(Feb.)	LARVA	LEPIDOPTERA Geometridae	*Operophtera fagata*	Northern winter moth	All ages	XXX	138 141 140
May to June Adult Oct./ Nov. & Feb.	LARVA	LEPIDOPTERA Geometridae	*Erannis defoliaria* Plate 33	Mottled umber moth	All ages	XX	118
May to June Adult Oct./ Dec.	LARVA	LEPIDOPTERA Geometridae	*Agriopis aurantiaria*	Scarce umber moth	All ages	XX	118
May Adult Aug./ Oct.	LARVA	LEPIDOPTERA Geometridae	*Epirrita autumnata*	Autumnal moth	All ages	XX	118
July to Sept. Adult May/ June/July	LARVA	LEPIDOPTERA Geometridae	*Biston betularia*	Peppered moth	All ages	XX	118
May to June	LARVA	LEPIDOPTERA Geometridae	*Apocheima pilosaria* (*Phigalia pedaria*) Plate 10	Pale brindled beauty moth	All ages	XX	118

PART OF TREE	DESCRIPTION OF DAMAGE AND FEEDING HABIT	DESCRIPTION OF DAMAGING STAGE *(see note on p.12)*
LEAF & BUD	Feeds as a clutch on the upper surfaces of leaves when young, within a silk tent. Overwinters as a larva and chews buds and leaves the following spring. Completely defoliates and can kill after repeated attacks. Prefers rosaceous species. Sheds extremely irritant hairs. Endemic on the S and SE coast and in the London area.	At first dark brown with two orange warts. Later covered in hairs and with two white lines of hair tufts down back. *c.*20mm.
LEAF	First stage larvae feed solitarily, later ones as a clutch protected by a silk tent. Can completely defoliate. Overwinters in egg clutches.	Ground colour blue. Down back a blueish-white stripe, on each side a reddish one and below this a reddish-orange one with flecks of orange under. 50mm.
LEAF	Four from a large genus of leaf-feeding weevils which can completely defoliate. Larvae feed on roots of a wide range of herbaceous and woody plants.	(1) Black with greenish-gold scales. 5–8mm. (2) & (3) Bright greenish or golden yellow. 5–6mm. (4) Dark brown with green head and whitish-brown scales. 3–4mm.
LEAF TWIG & STEM	Female secretes a large blob of waxy wool on stems and branches in which she lays abundant eggs. Most common in towns on *Aesculus*, *Tilia* and *Acer*.	Small very flattened, light brown to straw-coloured scale on leaves. 0.5mm.
STEM	Common on stressed trees of smooth-barked species. The wool under which the female lays eggs persists and is an obvious feature. Eggs and larvae are pink.	Small, pink, rather featureless. 0.5mm. Female scale mussel-shaped. Male less common, smaller and parallel-sided.
WOOD	First tunnels between bark and wood, later straighter in wood. Attacks old and debilitated trees. Ejects cylindrical wads of frass from base of tree and closes hole. Usually 2 years in wood.	Yellow-white larva with black dots. Head black. 40mm.
WOOD	Ramifying tunnels in wood of dead and dying trees. A great deal of foul smelling frass ejected from hole at base of stem. Up to 3-year cycle.	Very large larva, dark purple-red on back, yellow beneath. Head black. 75mm.
WOOD	Bores wandering black tunnels in the wood of trees often severely root-damaged through flooding, drought or fungi. Attacks still green trees and is probably the most aggressive 'ambrosia' beetle in UK.	Adult black to dark brown, flattened. Male smaller, rounded, 2–2.7mm; female longer, 3–3.5mm.

TIME OF DAMAGE	STAGE	ORDER AND FAMILY	LATIN NAME	ENGLISH NAME	TYPE OF CROP	DAMAGE RATING *(see key p.12)*	REFER-ENCE
Aug. to June Adult July/ Aug.	LARVA	LEPIDOPTERA Lymantriidae	*Euproctis chrysorrhoea* Plate 34	Browntail moth	Young and bush	XXXX	127
April to June Adult July/ Aug.	LARVA	LEPIDOPTERA Lasiocampidae	*Malacosoma neustria*	Lackey moth	Young and bush	XXX	5
April to July	ADULT & LARVA	COLEOPTERA Curculionidae	(1) *Phyllobius pyri* (2) & (3) *Phyllobius argentatus* and *P. roboretanus* (4) *Phyllobius viridicollis*	Common leaf weevil	All ages	XXX	117
May to Sept. (wax all year round)	NYMPH & ADULT	HEMIPTERA Coccidae	*Pulvinaria regalis* Plate 65	Horse chestnut scale	All ages	XX	126
May to June (wax all year round)	NYMPH & ADULT	HEMIPTERA Coccidae	*Chionaspis salicis*	Willow scale	All ages	XX	65
All year round Adult June/ Aug.	LARVA	LEPIDOPTERA Cossidae	*Zeuzera pyrina*	Leopard moth	All ages	XXX	109 65
All year round Adult June/ July	LARVA	LEPIDOPTERA Cossidae	*Cossus cossus*	Goat moth	Older	X	109 65
June/Aug. Adults May to June	ADULT & LARVA	COLEOPTERA Scolytidae	*Xyleborus dispar* Plate 95	Broadleaved pinhole borer	Young to older	XXX	117

PART OF TREE	DESCRIPTION OF DAMAGE AND FEEDING HABIT	DESCRIPTION OF DAMAGING STAGE *(see note on p.12)*
WOOD	Larvae feed only between bark and wood. A traditional pest of tannery bark. Attacks fresh-felled wood. Usually 2-year cycle. Occasional pest of hazel walking stick stock.	Larva a longhorn. 24mm. Adult yellow/red but variable. 6–17mm.
WOOD	Larva feeds in cambium area of rotting wood. Two year cycle.	Larva a longhorn. 27mm. Adult covered in grey-mottled hairs with two or three strongly raised ridges down wing covers and two black transverse bands. 10–20mm.
WOOD	As above species.	Larva a longhorn. 34mm. Adult with close, oblique yellow bands across wing covers, outside these a large black patch. 12–20mm.
WOOD	Larvae feed at first under bark and into sapwood, later tunnel into sapwood. Two year cycle.	Larva a longhorn. 20mm. Adult a brownish beetle with startling yellow transverse bands, a central one arrowhead-shaped pointing towards head. 7–14mm.
WOOD	One of a group of rather similar looking striking longhorns, the adults of which are often seen feeding on flowers. Larvae are found in the rotting wood of a variety of tree species. The cycle is upwards of 3 years.	Larva a longhorn. 24mm. Adult wings yellow with usually four rather uneven transverse black bands somewhat tapering. 14–20mm.
WOOD	The tree species of 'Stag beetles' are all found in decaying broadleaved wood and stumps. The first is the largest beetle in Britain. They overlap the Longhorn beetle niche but the larvae are obviously different. The first two are more southerly and the third northerly in distribution.	Larvae resemble Cockchafers but less swollen at hind end. Cream, curved and wrinkled. Head brown. Up to 50mm. (1) Male with antler-like processes on head with dark brown wings. 50–75mm. (2) Resembles above without processes. 25–35mm. (3) Smaller male with rhinoceros-like horn on head. 12–16mm.
WOOD	Attacks cut broadleaved timber with sufficient 'pore' size and starch content. Produces very fine boremeal.	Larvae small, cream and curved. Adult reddish-brown to black, flattened and parallel sided.
WOOD	Bores into the dead wood of most tree and hedgerow plants. (Plywood, basketwork and wattle are very susceptible.)	Larvae small, cream, curved and slightly 'humped' concealing the head which points downwards. 5mm. Adult grey-reddish brown, cylindrical, thorax covering head like a monk's cowl. 6–7mm.

TIME OF DAMAGE	STAGE	ORDER AND FAMILY	LATIN NAME	ENGLISH NAME	TYPE OF CROP	DAMAGE RATING (see key p.12)	REFER-ENCE
Adults May/ July. Larvae all year	LARVA	COLEOPTERA Cerambycidae	*Phymatodes testaceus*	Tanbark borer	Newly felled	X (or XXXX?)	75
Adults May/ June	LARVA	COLEOPTERA Cerambycidae	*Rhagium inquisitor*		Rotting wood	X	75
Adults May/ June	LARVA	COLEOPTERA Cerambycidae	*Rhagium mordax*	Oak longhorn beetle	Rotting wood	X	75
Adults May/ June	LARVA	COLEOPTERA Cerambycidae	*Clytus arietis*	Wasp beetle	Dead wood	X	75
Adult in July/ Aug.	LARVA	COLEOPTERA Cerambycidae	*Strangalia maculata*		Wood	X	75
Adults June/ July Adults June Adults May/ June	LARVA	COLEOPTERA Lucanidae	(1) *Lucanus cervus* (2) *Dorcus parallelipipedus* (3) *Sinodendron cylindricum*	Stag beetle Lesser stag beetle Spiked pox beetle	Dead wood	X	117
Adult July/ Aug.	LARVA	COLEOPTERA Lyctidae	*Lyctus brunneus*	Powder post beetle	Fresh-sawn	XXXX	40
Adult June/ July	LARVA	COLEOPTERA Anobiidae	*Anobium punctatum*	Furniture beetle	Dead wood	X (or XXXX!)	40

PART OF TREE	DESCRIPTION OF DAMAGE AND FEEDING HABIT	DESCRIPTION OF DAMAGING STAGE *(see note on p.12)*

ACER (MAPLE)

LEAF	Aphids feed on undersides of leaves throughout the growing season. Great quantities of honeydew produced – a common urban nuisance. Flies and resettles when disturbed.	Large green aphis with long legs. All winged during summer.
LEAF	Green to red, woody, often hairy, globular galls on upper side of leaves, near main veins, often coalescing.	Tiny elongate mite.
LEAF	Often thousands of purple or green, small, globular, glossy galls on upper side of leaf. On sycamore.	Tiny elongate mite.
LEAF	Similar to above on field maple.	Tiny elongate mite.
LEAF	Light brown, hairy, irregular, concave, felted patches on underside of leaf, raised yellow-green patches on upper side.	Tiny elongate mite.

ALNUS (ALDER)

LEAF	Feeds on edges of leaves and can completely defoliate. Two generations a year.	Body colour green. 2nd and last segments orange-yellow. Black central line, two similar, broader each side and below lines of dots. Head black to dark brown. 18mm.
LEAF	Young larvae make characteristic curved mines between veins (likened to 'writing'). Later stages eat whole leaf leaving only the main vein. Maybe two generations. *A. rubra* particularly prone to attack.	First and last segments yellow. Broad, dark blackish-green back stripe, blue-green underneath. Head black. 20mm.
LEAF	Eats out chunks of leaves and may completely defoliate. Can be two generations.	Larva at first pale green, then with black and yellow dots and finally greenish-yellow with prominent black patches. 23mm.
LEAF	Larva mines end portions of leaf, starting at main vein. Pupa in the mine. Adult eats out 'shot holes'.	Very small weevil. Body reddish, head black. 2.5–3mm. Larva small, white and tapering. Head brown.
LEAF	Skeletonises leaves and eats out holes, leaving the midrib.	Adult brilliant metallic green or coppery-blue. 5–8mm. Larva blackish-green. 5–6mm.
WOOD	Tunnels into the wood of dead and dying trees.	Body colour cream. Assumes 'S' shape when removed. Head and hind spine yellow brown.

TIME OF DAMAGE	STAGE	ORDER AND FAMILY	LATIN NAME	ENGLISH NAME	TYPE OF CROP	DAMAGE RATING (see key p.12)	REFER-ENCE
Spring & summer	NYMPH & ADULT	HEMIPTERA Calliphididae	*Drepanosiphum plantanoidis*	Sycamore aphid	Pole & older	XXX	52
June to Nov.	MITE	ACARI Eriophyidae	*Aceria macrochela*	Maple leaf solitary-gall mite	All ages	X	70
June to autumn	MITE	ACARI Eriophyidae	*Aculops acericola*	Sycamore gall mite	All ages	X	70
June to autumn	MITE	ACARI Eriophyidae	*Artacris macrorhynchus* Plate 12	Maple bead-gall mite	All ages	X	70
Spring to autumn	MITE	ACARI Eriophyidae	*Eriophyes megalonyx*	Sycamore felted pouch-gall mite	All ages	X	70

June to July & Sept.	LARVA	HYMENOPTERA Tenthredinidae	*Nematus pavidus*	Lesser willow sawfly	All ages	XXX	119
June to Oct.	LARVA	HYMENOPTERA Tenthredinidae	*Hemichroa crocea*		All ages	XXX	119
June to Sept.	LARVA	HYMENOPTERA Tenthredinidae	*Croesus septentrionalis* Plate 22	Hazel sawfly	All ages	XX	119 109
May to July	LARVA ADULT	COLEOPTERA Curculionidae	*Rhynchaenus alni*	Alder leaf miner	All ages	XX	117
June to July	ADULT & LARVA	COLEOPTERA Chrysomelidae	*Chrysomela aenea*		All ages	XX	117
Most of the year	LARVA	COLEOPTERA Siricidae	*Xiphydria camelus*	Alder woodwasp	Older wood	X	119

PART OF TREE	DESCRIPTION OF DAMAGE AND FEEDING HABIT	DESCRIPTION OF DAMAGING STAGE *(see note on p.12)*

BETULA (BIRCH)

LEAF	Perhaps the commonest aphid on birch. Very active, flying out from the plant when disturbed and back again. Secretes blue-white wax wool. Causes yellowing.	Light green. Adult always winged.
LEAF	An active hopping insect, causing a yellowing of foliage. Excretes a copious frothy 'spittle'.	Uniformly yellowish.
LEAF	Common aphid causing yellowing of leaves.	Green with longitudinal rows of tubercles.
LEAF	Eats out chunks of leaves and may completely defoliate. Can be two generations.	Larva at first pale green, then with black and yellow dots and finally greenish yellow with prominent black patches. 23mm.
LEAF	Eats out chunks of leaves. Can defoliate.	At first grey-white covered in wax powder, finally body wrinkled blueish-green down back. Head light brown with darker half-moon patch. 45mm.
LEAF	Larvae skeletonise in early stages, later eat out chunks and can defoliate. Two generations a year.	Pale green larva except for 2nd and last two segments which are orange. Three black lines and tubercles below. 19mm.
LEAF	Young larvae make characteristic curved mines between veins (likened to 'writing'). Later stages eat whole leaf leaving only the main vein. Maybe two generations.	First and last segments yellow. Broad, dark blackish-green back stripe, blue-green underneath. Head black. 20mm.
LEAF	Larvae eat out kidney-shaped mines in leaves. At least two generations per year.	Light green, flattened and tapered to rear. Head light yellow-brown. 5mm.
LEAF	Part of the defoliating complex of 'winter moths'. Eats out chunks of leaves.	Golden green or apple green with a green head. Three light side lines; upper ones thin, lower one distinct. Spiracles light brown. 20–27mm.
LEAF	Together with next species the commonest cause of defoliation in Scotland. Easily confused with *O. brumata* below.	Yellow to reddish with brown lines down back. Purplish lines on sides, dark striped yellowish under. Head light brown. 25–35mm.
LEAF	As above.	Light green sometimes with grey stripe down back. Three white-yellow lines on each side, upper wider than in *O. brumata* (below). Head and spiracles black. 15–22mm.

TIME OF DAMAGE	STAGE	ORDER AND FAMILY	LATIN NAME	ENGLISH NAME	TYPE OF CROP	DAMAGE RATING (see key p.12)	REFER-ENCE
April to Oct.	NYMPH & ADULT	HEMIPTERA Callaphididae	*Euceraphis punctipennis*	Silver birch aphid	All ages	X	38
Spring/ summer	NYMPH & ADULT	HEMIPTERA Cicadellidae	*Alnetoidea alneti*		All ages	XXX	
Spring/ summer	NYMPH & ADULT	HEMIPTERA Callaphididae	*Betulaphis quadrituberculata*		All ages	X	38
June to Sept.	LARVA	HYMENOPTERA Tenthredinidae	*Croesus septentrionalis* Plate 22	Hazel sawfly	All ages	XX	109 119
Spring/ summer	LARVA	HYMENOPTERA Cephalcidae	*Trichiosoma lucorum*		All ages	XX	119
June to Aug.	LARVA	HYMENOPTERA Tenthredinidae	*Nematus melanaspis*	Gregarious poplar sawfly	All ages	XXX	119
June to Oct.	LARVA	HYMENOPTERA Tenthredinidae	*Hemichroa crocea*		All ages	XXX	119
June to Sept.	LARVA	HYMENOPTERA Tenthredinidae	*Fenusa pusilla*	Birch sawfly	All ages	XX	119
May. Adult Aug./ Oct.	LARVA	LEPIDOPTERA Geometridae	*Epirrita autumnata*	Autumnal moth	All ages	XX	138
May/June Adult Oct. & later	LARVA	LEPIDOPTERA Geometridae	*Agriopis aurantiaria*	Scarce umber moth	All ages	XX	118
May/June/July Adult Oct./ Dec.	LARVA	LEPIDOPTERA Geometridae	*Operophtera fagata*	Northern winter moth	All ages	XXX	138

BETULA (BIRCH)

PART OF TREE	DESCRIPTION OF DAMAGE AND FEEDING HABIT	DESCRIPTION OF DAMAGING STAGE *(see note on p.12)*
LEAF	A very common defoliator of many tree species.	Very similar to *O. fagata* above. A paler form is light green with a usually green head. A darker form is blackish-green and has head dark. The upper of the three side lines is thinner than in *O. fagata*. 15–22mm.
LEAF	Again a constituent of the defoliating complex.	Colour variable. Reddish-brown above. Yellow patches on sides of front segments. Also a black side line edged with interrupted white. Head brown. 25mm.
LEAF	Larva rolls leaves into a cone or 'poke'.	Body yellowish, shield black. Head yellowish or brown with some black at back.
LEAF	Larva rolls leaves into a tube, often spinning leaves together.	Body greenish, shield small darker. Head green, marbled, whitish down centre.
LEAF	Larva mines end portions of leaf, starting at main vein. Pupa in the mine. Adult eats out 'shot holes'.	Very small weevil. Body reddish, head black. 2.5–3mm. Larva small, white and tapering. Head brown.
LEAF	Four from a large genus of leaf-feeding weevils which can completely defoliate. Larvae feed on roots of a wide range of herbaceous and woody plants.	(1) Black with greenish-gold scales. 5–8mm. (2) & (3) Bright green or golden yellow. 5–6mm. (4) Dark brown with green head & whitish-brown scales. 3–4mm.
LEAF & BUD	Larvae skeletonise leaf undersides. Adults eat out holes in leaves and gnaw buds and young shoots. Possibly two generations.	Straw coloured beetle with black head & undersides. 4–6mm. Larva blackish green. 5–6mm.
STEM	Egg gallery longitudinal with a hooked curve at the end and often with short side branches. Outside a regular row of 'air holes' tracing the system inside. Larval galleries long. One generation a year. Secondary on dead and dying trees. Local to Scottish central highlands.	Adult large dark brown to black and shining. 4.5–7mm.
WOOD	Tunnels into the wood of dead and dying trees.	Body colour cream. Assumes 'S' shape when removed. Head and hind spine yellow brown.

TIME OF DAMAGE	STAGE	ORDER AND FAMILY	LATIN NAME	ENGLISH NAME	TYPE OF CROP	DAMAGE RATING (see key p.12)	REFER-ENCE
May/June. Adult Nov./ Dec.	LARVA	LEPIDOPTERA Geometridae	*Operophtera brumata* Plate 51	Winter moth	All ages	XXX	138
May/June Adult Oct./ Jan.	LARVA	LEPIDOPTERA Geometridae	*Erannis defoliaria* Plate 33	Mottled umber moth	All ages	XX	118
June to July	LARVA	HYMENOPTERA Pamphiliidae	*Pamphilius pallipes*		All ages	X	119
June to July	LARVA	HYMENOPTERA Pamphiliidae	*Pamphilius varius*		All ages	X	119
May to July	ADULT & LARVA	COLEOPTERA Curculionidae	*Rhynchaenus alni*	Alder leaf miner	All ages	XX	117
April to July	ADULT	COLEOPTERA Curculionidae	(1) *Phyllobius pyri* (2) & (3) *Phyllobius argentatus* and *P. roboretanus* (4) *Phyllobius viridicollis*	Common leaf weevil	All ages	XXX	117
May/June & July/Sept.	LARVA & ADULT	COLEOPTERA Chrysomelidae	*Lochmaea caprea*		All ages	XXX	139
June/July to spring	ADULT & LARVA	COLEOPTERA Scolytidae	*Scolytus ratzburgi*	Birch bark beetle	Older trees	X	117
Most of the year	LARVA	HYMENOPTERA Siricidae	*Xiphydria camelus*	Alder woodwasp	Older wood	X	119

PART OF TREE	DESCRIPTION OF DAMAGE AND FEEDING HABIT	DESCRIPTION OF DAMAGING STAGE *(see note on p.12)*

FAGUS (BEECH)

LEAF	Winged aphids on leaf undersides in May causing some distortion. Colonies grow and trails of wax and honeydew accumulate. Severe browning of the foliage and blackening by sooty moulds follow.	Pale yellow-green aphid with pale transverse bands.
LEAF	Sucks sap like an aphid. Leaves turn yellow and later chestnut brown.	Active and jumping yellow aphid-like.
LEAF	Adult feeding causes 'shot holes' in leaves in early spring. Larvae mine usually the distal third or so of leaf which browns and appears frosted.	Cream weevil larva with brown head. Adult a grey-black weevil. 2mm.
LEAF	Makes galls on veins of leaf upper side, at first yellow with white hairs, later red-brown and hairy.	Tiny white midge larva.
LEAF	Makes galls on veins of leaf upper side, shiny, sharply pointed, cone-shaped, green or bright yellow or reddish at tip. Interveinal browning adjacent to gall.	Tiny white midge larva.
LEAF	Rust red shallow felted 'pouch galls' between veins on undersides of leaves.	Tiny elongate mite.
SEED	Eats out contents of seed and packs with frass.	Whitish larva striped deep reddish-orange. Head brown, shield lighter.
STEM & BRANCH	Young scale feeds through the bark of stems and branches and develops to an adult. Associated with a *Nectria* fungal canker and a component of a syndrome causing death of large trees. White waxy wool conspicuous on single or groups of stems. Overwinters in cocoon and pupates in spring.	Tiny pale yellow, immobile coccid covered in waxy wool.
STEM	Egg gallery irregular in thin bark, longitudinal in thicker. Larval galleries wandering giving shapeless maze of interconnected tunnels. On dead or dying branches and twigs.	Small black bark beetle. 1.5–2mm.

TIME OF DAMAGE	STAGE	ORDER AND FAMILY	LATIN NAME	ENGLISH NAME	TYPE OF CROP	DAMAGE RATING (see key p.12)	REFER-ENCE
May to July peak	NYMPHS & ADULT	HEMIPTERA Callaphididae	*Phyllaphis fagi* Plate 58	Beech wooly aphid	All ages	XXX	38 52
May/July	NYMPHS & ADULT	HEMIPTERA Cicadellidae	*Fagocyba cruenta*	Beech leaf hopper	All ages	XX	148
May/June	ADULT & LARVA	COLEOPTERA Curculionidae	*Rhynchaenus fagi* Plate 67	Beech leaf miner	All ages	XXX	19
June to Sept.	LARVA	DIPTERA Cecidomyiidae	*Hartigiola annulipes*	Beech pouch – gall midge	All ages	X	70
July to Sept.	LARVA	DIPTERA Cecidomyiidae	*Mikiola fagi*	Beech pouch – gall midge	All ages	X	70
Summer	MITE	ACARI Eriophyidae	*Artacris macrorhynchus ferrugineus*	Beech bead – gall midge	All ages	X	70
Aug. to Oct.	LARVA	LEPIDOPTERA Tortricidae	*Cydia fagiglandana*	Beech seed moth	Seed-bearing	XXXX	43
June/July through year	NYMPH & ADULT	HEMIPTERA Coccidae	*Cryptococcus fagisuga* Plate 23	Felted beech coccus	Pole & older	XXX	143 145
June to Aug. Adult May/June	LARVA	COLEOPTERA Scolytidae	*Ernoporus fagi*		Young wood of older trees	X	117

PART OF TREE	DESCRIPTION OF DAMAGE AND FEEDING HABIT	DESCRIPTION OF DAMAGING STAGE *(see note on p.12)*

FRAXINUS (ASH)

LEAF	Rolls leaf margins into yellow or purple swollen tube-like gall. Retards shoot growth. A close relative *P. fraxini* has adult with a dark patterning on the wings.	Flat aphid-like with 'broad shoulders' and tapering to rear; yellow green when young. Adults with diaphanous wings.
SHOOT & BUD	Mines leaves when young buds and shoots later, overwintering under bark beneath bud. Reputed to be an important cause of forking in ash. A southerly species.	Dirty grey-streaked reddish-green larva. Head and shield black. 12mm.
STEM	The presence of this scale is marked by the small blobs of waxy wool which cover the female and larvae. The scale is typical of stressed trees and often appears when stems are suddenly relieved of neighbouring shelter.	Orange-red female. Reddish larvae.
STEM	A very common bark beetle on both ash and lilac. Egg-gallery two-armed, transverse with central brood chamber. Maturation feeding in 'bark roses' in young green stems, often associated with ash canker. The commonest of four related species on ash.	Adult black thickly covered with grey and black scales. 3mm.

ILEX (HOLLY)

LEAF	Blister-like swelling on leaf, yellowish with darker centre, caused by mining of larva.	Tiny white dipterous larva.

JUGLANS (WALNUT)

LEAF	Forms shining, convex swellings on upper surface of leaf. Underside cavity felted yellow and hairy. On walnut.	Tiny yellow-white elongate mite.

POPULUS (POPLAR)

LEAF	Attacked leaves hinge often at midrib and form a pouch-like gall, yellow-green suffused with red.	Yellowish grey/green to brown with much wax.
LEAF	Blackening of leaves after much honeydew and sooty moulds. Often in galls of *Taphrina aurea*.	Pale green, hairy aphids with dark green markings. Winged with black transverse bands.

TIME OF DAMAGE	STAGE	ORDER AND FAMILY	LATIN NAME	ENGLISH NAME	TYPE OF CROP	DAMAGE RATING *(see key p.12)*	REFER-ENCE
Late May/June	NYMPH & ADULT	HEMIPTERA Psyllidae	*Psyllopsis fraxinicola*	Ash leaf psyllid	Young to older	XX	116
Sept. through to May	LARVA	LEPIDOPTERA Yponomeutidae	*Prays fraxinella*	Ash bud moth	Thicket & older	XXX	65
July to March/April Present all year	NYMPH & ADULT	HEMIPTERA Coccidae	*Pseudochermes fraxini*	Ash scale	Pole	XXX	116
April/May to July & Aug. to April/May	ADULT & LARVA	COLEOPTERA Scolytidae	*Leperisinus varius* Plates 43 & 85	Ash bark beetle	Small to older	X	117
June/July to April/May	LARVA	DIPTERA Agromyzidae	*Phytomyza ilicis*	Holly leaf miner	All ages		106
Spring & summer	MITE	ACARI Eriophyidae	*Aceria erineus* Plate 1		All ages	X	116
May/June to Sept.	NYMPH & ADULT	HEMIPTERA Pemphigidae	*Thecabius affinis*	Poplar/buttercup aphid	All ages	X	109
Summer	NYMPH & ADULT	HEMIPTERA Chaitophoridae	*Chaitophorus leucomelas*		All ages	X	38

POPULUS (POPLAR)

PART OF TREE	DESCRIPTION OF DAMAGE AND FEEDING HABIT	DESCRIPTION OF DAMAGING STAGE *(see note on p.12)*
LEAF	An active hopping insect, causing a yellowing of foliage. Excretes a copious frothy 'spittle'.	Uniformly yellowish.
LEAF	Mines leaf, starting narrow on underside, broadening into upperside, packing frass into rows. Pupates in mine.	Very small midge larva, white with gut showing through. Two small teeth at hind end.
LEAF	Makes a long serpentine mine visible from both sides. Mine clean, silvery and snail-trail like. Two generations a year.	Small active granular whitish larva with black head. Hind end sharply tapering.
LEAF	Larvae skeletonise in early stages, later eat out chunks and can defoliate. Two generations a year.	Pale green larva except for 2nd and last two segments which are orange. Three black lines and tubercles below. 19mm.
LEAF	Feeds on edges of leaves and can completely defoliate. Two generations a year.	Body colour green. 2nd and last segments orange-yellow. Black central line; two similar, broader lines on each side. Lines of dots below. Head black to dark brown. 18mm.
LEAF	Young larvae feed on leaf edges, later eat out chunks. Two generations a year.	Blue-green except for first and last three segments which are red-brown. The whole dotted in black. 25mm.
LEAF	Larvae feed as a clutch side-by-side, skeletonising underside of leaf at first, later eat out chunks. Can be two generations.	Young larvae pale green, then pale yellow and finally orange with black dots. 20mm.
LEAF	Eats out chunks of leaves. Can defoliate.	At first grey-white covered in wax powder. Finally body wrinkled, blueish-green with white tubercles over legs down back. Head light brown with darker half-moon patch. 45mm.
LEAF & BUD	Adults eat out small holes on sides and surfaces of leaf and gnaw buds in spring. Larvae skeletonise leaves.	Wing cases green, blue or violet. Head copper or green. 2–3mm.
LEAF & SHOOT	Adult gnaws shoots. Larvae feed as a clutch, side-by-side skeletonising undersides.	Adults metallic, shining green or bronze. 5mm. Larvae dirty grey-brown. 4–5mm.
LEAF & SHOOT	Damage as above species.	Adults metallic, shining blue. 5mm. Larvae dirty grey-brown. 4–5mm.
LEAF	Adults eat out large chunks of leaf. Larvae feed as a clutch at first skeletonising both sides of leaf, later eat out chunks. Two generations a year. Can completely defoliate. Is a serious pest of aspen.	Larva cream with black warts on side, from which, on alarm, exudes retractible bubbles of repellent fluid. 12–15mm. Adult brick red with black tip to wing-cases. 12mm.

TIME OF DAMAGE	STAGE	ORDER AND FAMILY	LATIN NAME	ENGLISH NAME	TYPE OF CROP	DAMAGE RATING (see key p.12)	REFER-ENCE
Summer		HEMIPTERA Cicadellidae	*Alnetoidea alneti*		All ages	XXX	
June/July Sept./Aug.	LARVA	DIPTERA Agromyzidae	*Paraphytomyza populi*	Poplar leaf-mining midge	All ages	XX	119
May/June & Aug.	LARVA	LEPIDOPTERA Phyllocnistidae	*Phyllocnistis unipunctella*	Poplar leaf miner	All ages	XX	95
June to Aug.	LARVA	HYMENOPTERA Tenthredinidae	*Nematus melanaspis*	Gregarious poplar sawfly	All ages	XXX	119
June/July to Sept.	LARVA	COLEOPTERA Tenthredinidae	*Nematus pavidus*	Lesser willow sawfly	All ages	XXX	119
May to Oct.	LARVA	HYMENOPTERA Tenthredinidae	*Nematus salicis*	Large willow sawfly	All ages	XXX	119
July to Sept.	LARVA	HYMENOPTERA Tenthredinidae	*Trichiocampus viminalis*	Poplar sawfly	All ages	XXX	109 119
Spring/ summer	LARVA	HYMENOPTERA Cimbicidae	*Trichiosoma lucorum*		All ages	XX	119
May to Sept.	ADULT	COLEOPTERA Chrysomelidae	*Chalcoides aurata*	Willow flea beetle	All ages	XX	84 117
May to Sept.	ADULT & LARVA	COLEOPTERA Chrysomelidae	*Phyllodecta vitellinae* Plate 59	Brassy willow beetle	Stool beds & older	XXX	98 109
May to Sept.	ADULT & LARVA	COLEOPTERA Chrysomelidae	*Phyllodecta vulgatissima*	Blue willow beetle	Stool beds & older	XXX	98 109
May to Sept.	ADULT & LARVA	COLEOPTERA Chrysomelidae	*Chrysomela populi* Plate 19	Large red poplar leaf beetle	Thicket & coppice	XXX	109 65

POPULUS (POPLAR)

PART OF TREE	DESCRIPTION OF DAMAGE AND FEEDING HABIT	DESCRIPTION OF DAMAGING STAGE *(see note on p.12)*
LEAF	Larvae can completely defoliate. Overwinters as larvae in silk tubes.	Dark grey larva with pale yellow and white dots and three pairs bright red hairy warts. 40mm.
LEAF	Eats chunks from leaves and can completely defoliate.	Large green larva with white-edged, saddle-shaped, purple band down length. Two 'tails' at back with reddish whips. 50mm.
LEAF	Makes a green suffused pink rounded gall.	Tiny orange gall midge larva. 3–4mm.
LEAF PETIOLE	Forms a smooth, round or pear-shaped gall on petiole, yellow-green diffused with reddish. Particularly on *P. nigra*.	Grey aphid covered with waxy wool.
LEAF PETIOLE	Forms a red, yellow or green spiral gall on leaf petiole.	Brown-grey aphid covered in waxy wool.
SHOOT	Larva bores up terminal stem particularly of stool shoots and leaf stalks. Frass ejected from entry hole at leaf axil out of which the larva also rests with cover of frass granules.	Body light brown. Head black to brown-black, shield brown. 7–8mm.
TWIG	Feeds on two-year-old twigs in colonies all year round.	Large pale grey-green, hairy aphid covered in wax.
STEM & BRANCHES	Forms large wax-covered colonies in fissures down stem and branches. Can cause die-back and death of trees.	Pale yellow aphid when young, dark green later with dirty whitish wax.
STEM	Burrows very long, sinuous tunnels from branchwood down stem cambium causing a pith-fleck to show in cross-section and brown galleries in veneers. A serious cause of veneer degrade.	Very long thin white larva only 1mm wide but 15–30mm long.
YOUNG STEM WOOD	Swelling like plumber's joint together with horseshoe-scar in young shoots. Larva feeds in pith. Damage often occluded but shoots break at swelling.	Longhorn larva. 12mm.
WOOD	Tunnels first in cambium and later into wood ejecting coarse frass from hole at base.	Yellowish white long larva. 35mm.

TIME OF DAMAGE	STAGE	ORDER AND FAMILY	LATIN NAME	ENGLISH NAME	TYPE OF CROP	DAMAGE RATING (see key p.12)	REFER-ENCE
April to June	LARVA	LEPIDOPTERA Lymantriidae	*Leucoma salicis* Plate 44	White satin moth	All ages	XX	109 118
June to Sept.	LARVA	LEPIDOPTERA Notodontidae	*Cerura vinula*	Puss moth	All ages	XXX	109 118
May to June	LARVA	DIPTERA Cecidomyiidae	*Contarinia petioli*	Poplar gall midge	All ages	X	109 119
July to Aug.	NYMPH & ADULT	HEMIPTERA Pemphigidae	*Pemphigus bursarius* Plate 56	Poplar/lettuce root gall aphid	All ages	X (serious on lettuce)	134
June to Aug.	NYMPH & ADULT	HEMIPTERA Pemphigidae	*Pemphigus spyrothecae*	Poplar spiral-gall aphid	All ages	X	134
July to Sept.	LARVA	LEPIDOPTERA Tortricidae	*Gypsonoma aceriana* Plate 36		Stool beds	XX	43
Summer	NYMPH & ADULT	HEMIPTERA Aphididae	*Pterocomma populeum* Plate 64		All ages	X	
Summer–July peak	NYMPH & ADULT	HEMIPTERA Pemphigidae	*Phloeomyzus passerini*	Woolly poplar aphid	Pole & mature	XXXX	84
May to July	LARVA	DIPTERA Agromyzidae	*Agromyza* sp.	Poplar cambium midge	Pole & older	XXXXX	109
June for two years	LARVA	COLEOPTERA Cerambycidae	*Saperda populnea*	Small poplar longhorn beetle	Young wood	XXX	109
June/July for two years	LARVA	COLEOPTERA Cerambycidae	*Saperda carcharias*	Large poplar longhorn beetle	Older	X	109 117

PART OF TREE	DESCRIPTION OF DAMAGE AND FEEDING HABIT	DESCRIPTION OF DAMAGING STAGE *(see note on p.12)*
WOOD	Larva bores ramifying tunnels in cambium and wood. Causes death of stems and branches above attack. A pest of stool beds.	Adult with black ground. Hind third of wing covered with dense yellowish-white scales. These scales elsewhere with patches of black ones. Snout curved. 7–9mm. Larva yellowish-white. 9–10mm.
WOOD	Ramifying tunnels in wood and down roots. Frass ejected in large quantities from small holes at base of tree stem. More common in E. Anglia and probably largely replaced by *Sphecia bembeciformis* (Lunar hornet moth) elsewhere.	Yellowish cream larva with brown head and legs. 15mm.

PRUNUS (CHERRY)

LEAF	Rolls leaves longitudinally. On *Prunus padus*. Migrates to grasses and cereals.	Yellowish-green, plumpish aphid. Later generations covered in grey waxy wool.
LEAF & SHOOT	Nymphs feed on leaves and shoots causing them to curl and shoots to distort forming a rosette-like growth covered in sooty moulds growing on the honeydew. Is a serious check to growth and can cause die-back. On *Prunus cerasi*.	Shiny blackish brown.
LEAF	Larvae feed together in a web. Can completely strip a tree. On *Prunus padus*. A northern species.	Whitish grey larva with black dots. 16mm.

QUERCUS (OAK)

LEAF	Adult lays usually two concentric rings of eggs on underside of leaf. Her feeding shows as a yellow dot on upperside. Nymphs cause wilting, leaf turning dirty grey-mottled brown and finally black with honeydew.	Orange-yellow aphid.
LEAF	On leaf undersides.	Yellow-green aphid. Darker winged in summer. Antennae distinctly banded.
LEAF	Bends the flower stalk and aborts acorn. Also on leaves.	Reddish- or greenish-brown, flattened, broadly oval and thinly covered with white wax powder.

TIME OF DAMAGE	STAGE	ORDER AND FAMILY	LATIN NAME	ENGLISH NAME	TYPE OF CROP	DAMAGE RATING *(see key p.12)*	REFER-ENCE
May/June for up to two years	LARVA	COLEOPTERA Curculionidae	*Cryptorhynchus lapathi* Plate 24	Osier weevil	All ages	XXX	74 123
July for up to two years	LARVA	LEPIDOPTERA Sesiidae	*Sesia apiformis*	Hornet clear-wing moth	Pole & older	XX	94 109

TIME OF DAMAGE	STAGE	ORDER AND FAMILY	LATIN NAME	ENGLISH NAME	TYPE OF CROP	DAMAGE RATING	REFERENCE
Spring	NYMPH & ADULT	HEMIPTERA Aphididae	*Rhopalosiphum padi*	Bird cherry aphid	All ages	XX	38
March/April to June/July	NYMPH & ADULT	HEMIPTERA Aphididae	*Myzus cerasi*	Cherry blackfly	All ages	XXX	38
May to June	LARVA	LEPIDOPTERA Yponomeutidae	*Yponomeuta evonymella*	Bird cherry ermine moth	All ages	XXX	6

TIME OF DAMAGE	STAGE	ORDER AND FAMILY	LATIN NAME	ENGLISH NAME	TYPE OF CROP	DAMAGE RATING	REFERENCE
May to July	ADULT & NYMPH	HEMIPTERA Phylloxeridae	*Phylloxera glabra* Plate 60	Oak phylloxera	Young trees & thicket	XXX	24
Spring & summer	ADULT & NYMPH	HEMIPTERA Callaphididae	*Tuberculoides annulatus*	Oak leaf aphid	All ages	X	
Spring & summer	ADULT & NYMPH	HEMIPTERA Thelaxidae	*Thelaxes dryophila*		All ages	X	38

QUERCUS (OAK)

PART OF TREE	DESCRIPTION OF DAMAGE AND FEEDING HABIT	DESCRIPTION OF DAMAGING STAGE *(see note on p.12)*
LEAF	Larva usually folds rather than rolls leaf, fixing in position with silk. A very common cause of complete defoliation of oak. The tree reclothes itself with typically rose-tinted epicormic or lammas growth.	Greenish-grey with black dots. Head brown with black markings or black. 12mm.
LEAF	Larva rolls leaf obliquely from tip backwards.	Whitish-grey to dark bluish-grey. Head black, shield dark brown to black. 12mm.
LEAF	Larva rolls leaf longitudinally producing a tight cigar.	Greyish-green to dark green. Head and shield light brown. 12mm.
LEAF	Larvae feed as a clutch and strip branches of foliage.	Large yellow with black lines. Hairy. Head black. 45mm.
LEAF	Larvae feed as a clutch and skeletonise lower surface.	Cream, exuding yellowish slime. Head brownish yellow with hind ⅔rds blackish-brown. Tapering.
LEAF	Damage as above species.	Cream exuding yellowish slime. Head uniformly red-brown. Tapering.
LEAF	Rolls or folds leaf margins towards undersides at vein ends in *D. dryobia*, towards uppersides between veins in *D. volvens*.	Yellowish-white larva with green gut visible. 2–3mm.
LEAF	Alternates between leaves. Produces (1) a few gregarious, at first cream-green, 4mm, lipped disc-shaped galls with central pimple, on underside of leaf. Later gall develops a purple edge. (2) single green galls on leaf edge (or veins) causing an indentation in leaf shape.	Small gall wasp larva.
LEAF	Alternates between leaves. Produces (1) hundreds of golden-brown, 3mm, doughnut shaped galls on underside of leaf, covered in shiny golden hairs. (2) Small grey-green circular galls which form slight swellings with radiating markings on both sides of leaf.	Small gall wasp larva.
LEAF	Alternates between leaves and male flowers (or again leaves). Produces (1) hundreds of first yellow, 6mm, flat disc-shaped galls, centrally raised like 'chinaman's hat' on underside of leaf. Galls later reddish. (2) at first green, later reddish 'currants' on male flowers (occasionally on leaves).	Small gall wasp larva.

TIME OF DAMAGE	STAGE	ORDER AND FAMILY	LATIN NAME	ENGLISH NAME	TYPE OF CROP	DAMAGE RATING *(see key p.12)*	REFER-ENCE
May	LARVA	LEPIDOPTERA Tortricidae	*Tortrix viridana*	Oak leaf roller moth	Pole & older	XXX	153
April to June	LARVA	LEPIDOPTERA Tortricidae	*Archips xylosteana*	Brown oak tortrix	All ages	X	42
May to June	LARVA	LEPIDOPTERA Tortricidae	*Eudemis profundana*		All ages	X	43
May to June	LARVA	LEPIDOPTERA Notodontidae	*Phalera bucephela* Plate 57	Buff-tip moth	Thicket	X	118
June to Aug.		HYMENOPTERA Tenthredinidae	*Caliroa annulipes* Plate 17	Oak slug worm	All ages	X	119
Sept. to Oct.	LARVA	HYMENOPTERA Tenthredinidae	*Caliroa cinxia*	Oak slug worm	All ages	X	119
June	LARVA	DIPTERA Cecidomyiidae	*Macrodiplosis dryobia* and *M. volvens*	Leaf-roll gall midge	All ages	X	70 71
July to Oct. April to May	LARVA	HYMENOPTERA Cynipidae	*Neuroterus albipes*	Smooth spangle-gall wasp Schenk's gall wasp	All ages	X	7 70 71
Aug. to Sept. May to June	LARVA	HYMENOPTERA Cynipidae	*Neuroterus numismalis* Plate 48	Silk button-gall wasp Blister-gall wasp	All ages	X	7 70 71
July to Sept. April to June	LARVA	HYMENOPTERA Cynipidae	*Neuroterus quercus-baccarum* Plate 49	Common spangle-gall wasp Currant gall wasp	All ages	X	7 70 71

PART OF TREE	DESCRIPTION OF DAMAGE AND FEEDING HABIT	DESCRIPTION OF DAMAGING STAGE *(see note on p.12)*
LEAF	Alternates between leaves and buds. Produces globular galls of varying size but less than 1cm on underside on veins of leaves. Yellowish at first, red-brown later. (2) inconspicuous 'red wart' galls on buds.	Small gall wasp larva.
LEAF & BUD	Alternates between leaves and buds. Produces (1) spheroidal, bluntly pointed, pink to reddish, 7mm, galls on buds of young plants and epicormic shoots. (2) glossy, smooth, stalked, yellowish green to purple-brown kidney galls on underside of leaves, 2–3mm. These drop in October and overwinter.	Small gall wasp larva.
LEAF & BUD	Alternates between leaves and buds. Produces (1) red or mottled red cherry-sized galls, larger than 1cm on ribs of underside. (2) inconspicuous red to black, velvety galls on buds of side or epicormic shoots.	Small gall wasp larva.
LEAF & BUD	Alternates between leaf petiole and bud. Produces (1) a green swelling and distortion of petiole extending on to leaf main rib. (2) inconspicuous 'collared-bud', pear-shaped gall on bud.	Small gall wasp larva.
STEM & LEAF	Alternates between root-collar area and leaf. Produces (1) pinkish barnacle-like gall clustered at base of stem of nursery stock, natural regeneration and on callous tissue of damaged older stems. (2) inconspicuous green swellings on leaf veins and petioles.	Small gall wasp larva.
LEAF & BUD	Alternates between leaf veins and side buds. Produces (1) yellowish-green, pink or brown galls dotted red. (2) inconspicuous swollen bud galls.	Small gall wasp larva.
LEAF & BUD	Alternates between leaves of native oaks and buds of *Q. cerris* (Turkey oak). Produces (1) at first green, later hard and brown spherical galls clustered and often arising from leaf veins.	Small gall wasp larva.
BUD & MALE FLOWER	Alternates between bud and male flowers. Produces (1) at first green, later brown, soft, hop-shaped gall. (2) hairy catkin-like gall on male flowers.	Small gall wasp larva.

TIME OF DAMAGE	STAGE	ORDER AND FAMILY	LATIN NAME	ENGLISH NAME	TYPE OF CROP	DAMAGE RATING *(see key p.12)*	REFER- ENCE
Sept. to Oct. Oct./May– June	LARVA	HYMENOPTERA Cynipidae	*Cynips divisa*	Red-pea gall wasp Red-wart gall wasp	All ages	X	70
(1) Late winter to May/June (2) June/July to Sept./ Oct.	LARVA	HYMENOPTERA Cynipidae	*Trigonaspis megaptera*	Pink bud gall wasp Kidney-gall wasp	Young plants & epicormics	X	70
July to winter April/May	LARVA	HYMENOPTERA Cynipidae	*Cynips quercusfolii*	Cherry gall wasp A bud gall wasp	All ages	X	70
July to Sept. April/May	LARVA	HYMENOPTERA Cynipidae	*Andricus curvator*	Curved-leaf gall wasp Collared-bud gall wasp	All ages	X	70
Aug./Sept. for two years May to Aug.	LARVA	HYMENOPTERA Cynipidae	*Andricus testaceipes*	Red-barnacle gall wasp A leaf gall wasp	All ages	X	70 71
June to Oct. April	LARVA	HYMENOPTERA Cynipidae	*Andricus anthracina* (*A. ostria*)	Oyster gall wasp A bud gall wasp	All ages	X	70
Summer to autumn Spring	LARVA	HYMENOPTERA Cynipidae	*Andricus kollari*	Oak marble gall wasp A bud gall wasp	All ages	X	70 71
June to Sept. April to May	LARVA	HYMENOPTERA Cynipidae	*Andricus fecundator* Plate 7	Artichoke or hop gall wasp Catkin gall wasp	All ages	X	70 71

PART OF TREE	DESCRIPTION OF DAMAGE AND FEEDING HABIT	DESCRIPTION OF DAMAGING STAGE *(see note on p.12)*
BUD & ROOTS	Alternates between buds and roots. Produces (1) whitish-green, often blushed pink, soft, unevenly globular gall containing many larvae. (2) roundish brown galls, often clustered on roots.	Small gall wasp larva.
ACORN & MALE FLOWER	Alternates between acorns of native oaks and *Q. cerris* (Turkey oak). Produces (1) a gross distortion of acorns and cup. Green and sticky at first turning brown and woody. (2) inconspicuous green cone-shaped gall on male flowers of *Q. cerris*.	Small gall wasp larva.
ACORN	Egg laid in developing nut or acorn. Larva eats contents and causes premature fall. Emerging adult leaves round hole. Adults feed a little on buds and opening shoots making holes.	Larva a small weevil type. Adult very long snouted, heavily grey-scaled on black ground. Often with yellower scales in vague transverse bands. 6–9mm. Hairs down inner edges of wings.
ACORN	Egg laid when acorn reaches about 1cm diameter. Larva eats out contents and causes early fall. Adult leaves round hole.	Larva a small weevil type. Adult very long snouted, covered with greyish-yellow to light brown scales on black ground. 4–8mm. No hairs down inner edges of wings.
ACORN	Larva eats out contents of nut.	Greyish-green to yellow-white. Head yellow-brown.
YOUNG STEM	Aphid sucks through the stem. No obvious damage but plenty of honeydew. Attended by ants.	Large dark brown aphid with long legs. Winged adults with clouded wings.
YOUNG STEM	Causes die-back of 2nd-year branchlets. Patches of bark fissure and canker.	Small pale yellowish brown.
OLDER STEM	Locally common in poor oak on acid soils.	Dirty grey to blackish, flat, ovoid scale adpressed to stem.
STEM	Egg gallery transverse, two-armed, without any obvious brood chamber. Larval tunnels very long and vertical. Maturation feeding at base of young shoots or into buds. Appears to attack only trees with advanced root rot.	Pitchy brown, thorax shining black. 2.5–4mm.

TIME OF DAMAGE	STAGE	ORDER AND FAMILY	LATIN NAME	ENGLISH NAME	TYPE OF CROP	DAMAGE RATING (see key p.12)	REFER-ENCE
Winter to July July for up to two years	LARVA	HYMENOPTERA Cynipidae	*Biorhiza pallida*	Oak apple gall wasp A root gall wasp	All ages	X	70 71
Spring to summer Winter to spring	LARVA	HYMENOPTERA Cynipidae	*Andricus quercuscalicis* Plate 8	Knopper gall wasp A flower gall wasp	Acorn bearers	XX	99
April to July/Sept.	LARVA	COLEOPTERA Curculionidae	*Curculio nucum* Plate 25	Nut weevil	Fruit bearers	XX	45 117
May to June/Sept.	LARVA	COLEOPTERA Curculionidae	*Curculio glandium*		Fruit bearers	XX	45 96
Aug./May	LARVA	LEPIDOPTERA Tortricidae	*Cydia splendana*	Acorn moth	Fruit bearers	XXXX	43
May to Oct.	NYMPH & ADULT	HEMIPTERA Lachnidae	*Lachnus roboris*		Pole & younger	X	
Spring to summer	NYMPH & ADULT	HEMIPTERA Phylloxeridae	*Moritziella corticalis* Plate 46	Oak bark phylloxera	Up to 10 years	XXX	24
May/Sept.	NYMPH & ADULT	HEMIPTERA Coccidae	*Kermes quercus*	Oak scale or pox	Pole stage	XXX	116
April to Aug.	ADULT & LARVA	COLEOPTERA Scolytidae	*Scolytus intricatus* Plate 91	Oak bark beetle	Pole to older	s	89 117

PART OF TREE	DESCRIPTION OF DAMAGE AND FEEDING HABIT	DESCRIPTION OF DAMAGING STAGE *(see note on p.12)*
STEM	Egg gallery more than one-armed, irregular, sometimes star-like, within the bark. Bore dust a very fine brown powder.	Dark brown to black, covered in long yellow hairs. 2.5–3.5mm.
ROOT & TWIG	Produces (1) potato-shaped, often large yellow-red or brown galls just below surface of soil on fine roots. 3–6cm. (2) very inconspicuous 'knot galls' on young stems; a small pale area on green twig stems.	Curved gall wasp larva.
WOOD	Bores a 2, 3 or 4-branched and blackened system in sapwood. Piles of white bore-meal obvious. A very close relative of *X. signatus*, also on oak.	Adult black or dark brown with yellow-orange stripes on wing covers. Head and thorax black. 3–4mm.
WOOD	Bores into sapwood, at first radially, then wandering, branched tunnels deeper into heartwood.	Larva cream. Head dark brown, banded at back. Adult oblong, black or dark brown. 5–5.5mm.
VERY OLD WOOD	Bores into long dead oak. Typical of ancient hollow oaks. Emergence holes much larger than Furniture beetle with which it is often found. Holes 3mm. Attacks persist up to 3 or 4 years.	Larva very similar to a bark beetle but with three pairs of legs. Beetle chocolate brown, covered with patches of yellowish hairs. Thorax flanged. 6–8mm.

SALIX (WILLOW)

LEAF	An active hopping insect, causing a yellowing of foliage.	Uniformly yellowish.
LEAF	Feeds as a colony of nymphs upon xylem sap of a number of broadleaved trees, within large blobs of froth. When feeding actively the froth drips. *A. salicina*, a unicolourous, pale brown relation is less common and confined to sallow. Both overwinter as eggs.	Dark brown bug with fawn saddle markings. Head pointed. 8mm.
LEAF	Larvae skeletonise leaves in early stages, later eat out chunks and can defoliate. Two generations a year.	Pale green larvae except for 2nd and last two segments which are orange. Three black lines and tubercles below. 19mm.
LEAF	Feeds on edges of leaves and can completely defoliate. Two generations a year.	Body colour green with 2nd and last segments orange-yellow. Black central line, two similar, broader lines on each side. Lines of dots below. Head black to dark brown. 18mm.

TIME OF DAMAGE	STAGE	ORDER AND FAMILY	LATIN NAME	ENGLISH NAME	TYPE OF CROP	DAMAGE RATING (see key p.12)	REFER-ENCE
May/July to April/Aug.	LARVA	COLEOPTERA Scolytidae	*Dryocoetinus villosus*		Older & logs	s	117
(1) All year round (2) April to mid-summer	LARVA	HYMENOPTERA Cynipidae	*Andricus quercusradicis*	Truffle gall wasp	All ages	XX	70
June/July	LARVA & ADULT	COLEOPTERA Scolytidae	*Xyloterus domesticus* Plate 96	Broad-leaved ambrosia beetle	Logs	s	117
July to Sept.	ADULT & LARVA	COLEOPTERA Platypodidae	*Platypus cylindrus* Plate 98	Oak pinhole borer	Logs	s	10 11
Adult–July/ Aug. for 2, 3, 4 years	ADULT & LARVA	COLEOPTERA Anobiidae	*Xestobium rufovillosum*	Death watch beetle	Ancient wood	s	40

Summer	ADULT & NYMPH	HEMIPTERA Cicadellidae	*Alnetoidea alneti*		All ages	XXX	
June to mid-Aug.	NYMPH	HEMIPTERA Cercopidae	*Aphrophora alni*	Broadleaf spittle bug	All ages	XX	108 116
June to Aug.	LARVA	HYMENOPTERA Tenthredinidae	*Nematus melanaspis*	Gregarious poplar sawfly	All ages	XXX	119
June to July and Sept.	LARVA	HYMENOPTERA Tenthredinidae	*Nematus pavidus*	Lesser willow sawfly	All ages	XX	119

PART OF TREE	DESCRIPTION OF DAMAGE AND FEEDING HABIT	DESCRIPTION OF DAMAGING STAGE *(see note on p.12)*
LEAF	Young larvae on leaf edges, later eat out chunks. Two generations a year.	Blue-green except for first and last three segments which are red-brown. The whole dotted in black. 25mm.
LEAF	Larvae feed as a clutch side-by-side, skeletonising underside of leaf at first, later eat out chunks. Can be two generations.	Young larvae pale green, then pale yellow and finally orange with black dots. 20mm.
LEAF	Eats out chunks of leaves. Can defoliate.	At first grey-white covered in wax powder. Finally body wrinkled blueish-green down back. Head light brown with darker half-moon patch. 45mm.
LEAF	Skeletonises leaves and eats out holes, leaving the midrib.	Adult brilliant metallic green or coppery-blue. 58mm. Larvae blackish when young, later lighter with black dots. Head and shield black. 10mm.
LEAF & BUD	Larvae skeletonise leaf undersides. Adults eat out holes in leaves and gnaw buds and young shoots. Possibly two generations.	Straw coloured beetle with black head and undersides. 4–6mm. Larva blackish-green. 5–6mm.
STEM & TWIG	Larvae skeletonise leaves and feed on twigs. Adults gnaw holes in leaves and eat young bark and terminal buds. Can completely defoliate and cause die-back of branches. Common on *S. amygdalina*.	Adults straw yellow. 5mm. Larvae pale yellow with black central and side stripes. Head and thorax black.
LEAF & BUD	Adult eats out small holes on sides and surface of leaf and gnaws buds in spring. Larvae skeletonise leaves.	Wing cases green, blue or violet. Head copper or green. 2–3mm.
LEAF & SHOOT	Adult gnaws shoots. Larvae feed together, side-by-side, skeletonising underside. Common on *S. purpurea*. Two broods a year.	Adults metallic, shining green or bronze. 5mm. Larvae dirty grey-brown. 4–5mm.
LEAF & SHOOT	Damage as above species. Common on *S. viminalis*. Two broods a year.	Adults metallic, shining blue. 5mm. Larvae dirty grey-brown. 4–5mm.
LEAF & SHOOT	Adult gnaws shoots and buds. Larvae skeletonise leaves from lower side. Two or more generations in the year.	Adults metallic blue, green or coppery. Rounder than above species. 2.5–5mm. Larvae dark grey with rows of black warts. 5mm.
LEAF	Eats chunks from leaves and can completely defoliate.	Large green larva with white-edged, saddle-shaped, purple band down length. Two 'tails' at back with reddish whips. 70mm.

TIME OF DAMAGE	STAGE	ORDER AND FAMILY	LATIN NAME	ENGLISH NAME	TYPE OF CROP	DAMAGE RATING (see key p.12)	REFER- ENCE
May to Oct.	LARVA	HYMENOPTERA Tenthredinidae	Nematus salicis	Large willow sawfly	All ages	XX	119
July to Sept.	LARVA	HYMENOPTERA Tenthredinidae	Trichiocampa viminalis	Poplar sawfly	All ages	XXX	109 119
Spring/ summer	LARVA	HYMENOPTERA Cimbicidae	Trichiosoma lucorum		All ages	XX	119
June to July	ADULT & LARVA	COLEOPTERA Chrysomelidae	Chrysomela aenea		All ages	XX	117
May/June & July/Sept.	ADULT & LARVA	COLEOPTERA Chrysomelidae	Lochmaea caprea		All ages	XXX	117
Mid-June & Aug.	ADULT & LARVA	COLEOPTERA Chrysomelidae	Galerucella lineola	Brown willow beetle	All ages	XXX	97
May/Aug.	ADULT	COLEOPTERA Chrysomelidae	Chalcoides aurata	Willow flea beetle	All ages	XX	84 117
May/Sept.	ADULT & LARVA	COLEOPTERA Chrysomelidae	Phyllodecta vitellinae Plate 59	Brassy willow beetle	Stool beds & older	XXX	98 65
May/Sept.	ADULT & LARVA	COLEOPTERA Chrysomelidae	Phyllodecta vulgatissima	Blue willow beetle	Stool beds & older	XXX	98 65
May/June to Sept./Oct.	LARVA & ADULT	COLEOPTERA Chrysomelidae	Plagiodera versicolora	Broader willow leaf beetle	All ages	XXX	117
June to Sept.	LARVA	LEPIDOPTERA Notodontidae	Cerura vinula	Puss moth	All ages	XXX	118

PART OF TREE	DESCRIPTION OF DAMAGE AND FEEDING HABIT	DESCRIPTION OF DAMAGING STAGE *(see note on p.12)*
LEAF	Larvae can completely defoliate. Overwinter as larvae in silk tubes.	Black larva with white or pale yellow spots down back and a yellow side stripe with orange-red hairy warts above and below it. 40–45mm.
LEAF	Hard yellow/green turning red, coffee bean-sized gall with small hole and extending both sides of leaf. Two generations a year.	Pale, greyish yellow-green sawfly. Head black-brown. 9mm.
LEAF	Hard yellow-green to pink, round or oval gall on underside near midrib. Two generations a year.	Pale whitish green sawfly. Head yellow-brown. 12–13mm.
YOUNG SHOOT	Feeds in colonies on 2-year-old shoots.	Grey-black with white spots or patches, bright orange-red legs and cornicles.
YOUNG STEM & TWIGS	A very large aphid which feeds on the stem, branches and twigs in large colonies. May cause die-back of crown parts. Wood often brown stained under feeding.	Large dark grey, covered with regularly placed black speckles.
YOUNG STEM WOOD	Swelling like plumber's joint together with horseshoe-scar on young shoots or withies. Larva feeds in pith. Damage often occluded but shoots break at swelling.	Longhorn larva. 12mm.
WOOD	Tunnels first in cambium and later into wood ejecting coarse frass from hole at base of stem.	Yellowish white longhorn larva. 35mm.
WOOD	Larva bores ramifying tunnels in cambium and wood. Causes death of stems and branches above attack. Serious pest of osier beds.	Adult with black ground. Hind third of wing covers with dense yellowish-white scales. These scales elsewhere with patches of black ones. Snout curved. 7–9mm. Larva yellowish-white. 9–10mm.
WOOD	Larva bores first between bark and wood, later into wood. In branches and stems, particularly in trees liable to flood. Two year cycle.	Longhorn up to 35mm. Adult bright green or bluish-green. Wing-cases with two or three raised lines. 20–30mm.

SORBUS (ROWAN etc.)

LEAF	Causes a die-back of the shoots due to feeding and wilt of leaves. Alternates on narrow-leaved plantain.	Pale translucent greyish or grey-green. Winged slightly pinkish. A great deal of wax present.

TIME OF DAMAGE	STAGE	ORDER AND FAMILY	LATIN NAME	ENGLISH NAME	TYPE OF CROP	DAMAGE RATING *(see key p.12)*	REFER-ENCE
July/Aug. to May/June	LARVA	LEPIDOPTERA Lymantriidae	*Leucoma salicis* Plate 44	White satin moth	All ages	XX	109 118
June/July & Aug./Sept.	LARVA	HYMENOPTERA Tenthredinidae	*Pontania proxima*	Willow bean-gall sawfly	All ages	X	119
June to Aug.	LARVA	HYMENOPTERA Tenthredinidae	*Pontania viminalis*	Willow pea-gall sawfly	All ages	X	65 119
Summer	NYMPH & ADULT	HEMIPTERA Aphididae	*Pterocomma salicis* Plate 64	Black willow aphid	All ages	X	109
Summer	NYMPH & ADULT	HEMIPTERA Lachnidae	*Tuberolachnus salignus*	Large willow aphid	All ages	XX	109
June for two years	LARVA	COLEOPTERA Cerambycidae	*Saperda populnea*	Small poplar longhorn beetle	Young wood	XXX	109 117
June/July for two years	LARVA	COLEOPTERA Cerambycidae	*Saperda carcharias*	Large poplar longhorn beetle	Older	X	109 116
May/June for up to two years	LARVA	COLEOPTERA Curculionidae	*Cryptorhynchus lapathi* Plate 24	Osier weevil	All ages	XXX	74 123
All year round Adult June/ Sept.	LARVA	COLEOPTERA Cerambycidae	*Aromia moschata*	Musk beetle	Pole & older	XX	75

| May to June | NYMPH & ADULT | HEMIPTERA Aphididae | *Dysaphis aucupariae* Plate 30 | Wild service aphid | All ages | XXX | 38 |

PART OF TREE	DESCRIPTION OF DAMAGE AND FEEDING HABIT	DESCRIPTION OF DAMAGING STAGE *(see note on p.12)*
LEAF	Pale green, red to reddish-brown, shiny pustules coalescing in patches on both sides of leaves and petiole. On *Sorbus aucuparia*.	Tiny elongate mite.
SEED	Can destroy high proportion of seed particularly in western districts. On *Sorbus*, *Pyrus* and *Malus* species.	Gall wasp larva.

TILIA (LIME)

LEAF	Aphid present on leaves throughout late spring and summer, always winged. Produces copious honeydew.	Yellow-green or yellow with black markings.
LEAF	Outbreaks are always sudden and dramatic. The mite moves from tree bases in spring to the leaves, spinning sheets of silk which clothe the tree in a sheath. This breaks up and disperses with mites. Leaves turn dirty grey-brown. Massive premature leaf fall about August.	Tiny orange-red mite.
LEAF	Makes a greenish yellow to reddish-brown gall, conical, straight or curved looking like 'rusty tacks' on upper surface.	Tiny elongate mite.
LEAF	Larvae feed as a clutch and strip branches of foliage.	Large, yellow with black lines. Hairy. Head black. 45mm.

ULMUS (ELM)

LEAF	Smooth, stalked, conical, bladder-like gall. Yellow-green sometimes suffused pink. Opens to release aphids through small slit at base; migrate to grasses.	Blackish aphid with mealy grey abdomen.
LEAF	One side of leaf swells causing leaf to roll. Contains aphids and wool. Gall yellow-green turning pink then grey. Gall unrolls to release aphids; migrate to currants.	Yellow-green to brownish.
LEAF	Larvae feed as a clutch and strip branches of foliage.	Large, yellow with black lines. Hairy. Head black. 45mm.

TIME OF DAMAGE	STAGE	ORDER AND FAMILY	LATIN NAME	ENGLISH NAME	TYPE OF CROP	DAMAGE RATING (see key p.12)	REFER-ENCE
May to Aug.	MITE	ACARI Eriophyidae	*Aculus aucuparia*	Rowan gall mite	Young to older	X	70
April	LARVA	HYMENOPTERA Torymidae	*Torymus druparum*	Wild service seed wasp	Seed-bearing	XX	150

TIME OF DAMAGE	STAGE	ORDER AND FAMILY	LATIN NAME	ENGLISH NAME	TYPE OF CROP	DAMAGE RATING	REFER-ENCE
June to Sept.	NYMPH & ADULT	HEMIPTERA Callaphididae	*Eucallipterus tiliae*	Lime aphid	All ages	XXX	38 56
June to Sept.	MITE	ACARI Tetranychidae	*Eotetranychus tiliarium*	Lime mite	Pole & older	XXX	48
June to Aug.	MITE	ACARI Eriophyidae	*Eriophyes tiliae*	Lime nail gall mite	All ages	X	38
May to June	LARVA	LEPIDOPTERA Notodontidae	*Phalera bucephela* Plate 57	Buff-tip moth	Thicket	X	118

TIME OF DAMAGE	STAGE	ORDER AND FAMILY	LATIN NAME	ENGLISH NAME	TYPE OF CROP	DAMAGE RATING	REFER-ENCE
May to July	NYMPH & ADULT	HEMIPTERA Pemphigidae	*Tetraneura ulmi* Plate 70	Elm leaf gall aphid	All ages	X	70
June	NYMPH & ADULT	HEMIPTERA Pemphigidae	*Eriosoma ulmi*	Elm leaf aphid	All ages	X	38 52
May to June	LARVA	LEPIDOPTERA Notodontidae	*Phalera bucephela* Plate 57	Buff-tip moth	Thicket	X	118

PART OF TREE	DESCRIPTION OF DAMAGE AND FEEDING HABIT	DESCRIPTION OF DAMAGING STAGE *(see note on p.12)*
STEM & TWIG	Egg galleries up to 10cm and larval 15cm, the system forming an oval pattern. Maturation feeding in twig crotches, young wood as well as in the cambium prior to egg-laying. Pupates in radially cut cells in bark, rarely into wood. An important vector of Dutch elm disease. Overwinters as larva.	Head and thorax shining black, wing covers pitchy red-brown. 5–6mm.
STEM & TWIG	Very similar to above but smaller system. Egg gallery 2–6cm, larval 2–6cm. Maturation feeding as above but pupation at larval gallery end. Overwinters as larva.	Description superficially similar to above, smaller. 2.5–3.5mm.
STEM & TWIG	Again similar to above species. Egg gallery longitudinal with a distinct boot-shaped brood chamber at base, 4–10cm, larval 8cm. Pupates in radially cut cells in the wood. Outside surface of bark with diagnostic row of 'air holes' immediately above egg gallery. Maturation as above species. Recent introduction now spread from Cheshire and Yorkshire to Edinburgh.	Description superficially similar to above. 3.5–4.5mm.
BRANCH	In dead branches of 15cm or more diameter. Gallery a star of radiating larval galleries from a central egg chamber. Very common on Dutch elm diseased trees.	A small black weevil with long curved snout. 2.5–4.5mm.
BRANCH	Attacks only small diameter dead or dying branchlets in UK. Egg gallery two-armed and transverse, larval wandering. Maturation feeding and overwintering in canker-like 'bark roses' in thin bark.	Black, cylindrical beetle covered in ashy-grey scales. 1.5–2mm.
STEM	A native of Canada and USA. Usually two-armed egg gallery with central brood chamber mostly in the bark but may score wood. Maturation and sometimes overwintering in separate borings into bark but can overwinter as a larva in gallery. Attacks dead and dying elm of 5cm and over.	Brownish black beetle thinly clothed in stiff yellow hair. 2.5–3cm.

TIME OF DAMAGE	STAGE	ORDER AND FAMILY	LATIN NAME	ENGLISH NAME	TYPE OF CROP	DAMAGE RATING *(see key p.12)*	REFER-ENCE
April/May to July & Aug./ Sept. to April/May	ADULT & LARVA	COLEOPTERA Scolytidae	*Scolytus scolytus* Plates 68 and 93 See also p.121	Large elm beetle	Pole to older	XXXXX or S	46 83 88 100 122
Mid-June to July	ADULT & LARVA	COLEOPTERA Scolytidae	*Scolytus multistriatus* Plate 92 See also p.121	Small elm beetle	Pole to older	XXXXX or S	46 88 122
Probably as *S. scolytus*	ADULT & LARVA	COLEOPTERA Scolytidae	*Scolytus laevis* See also p.121		Pole to older	? or s	8 103 117
April/May to July	ADULT & LARVA	COLEOPTERA Curculionidae	*Magdalis armigera*				117
All year round	ADULT & LARVA	COLEOPTERA Scolytidae	*Acrantus vittatus* Plate 75		Pole & older	s	80
May through spring and summer	ADULT & LARVA	COLEOPTERA Scolytidae	*Hylurgopinus rufipes** Plate 80	Native bark beetle	Pole & older	XXXXX or S	146

PART OF TREE	DESCRIPTION OF DAMAGE AND FEEDING HABIT	DESCRIPTION OF DAMAGING STAGE *(see note on p.12)*

NURSERY

PART OF TREE	DESCRIPTION OF DAMAGE AND FEEDING HABIT	DESCRIPTION OF DAMAGING STAGE
GERMINAT-ING & EMERGENT SEEDLING	Attacks germinating seed and young plants, resulting either in death below ground, damage to the hypocotyl or a bushy-topped seedling with thickened, distorted cotyledons. Subsequent year's growth produces a multi-leadered cull. *P. contorta* appears particularly susceptible.	Tiny, grey-black, jumping flea-like insects without wings.
NEEDLE	Webs the needles of the shoot tip and sometimes nearby seedlings together. Feeds on the needles which turn brown. The main bud may abort but recovery is normally good. One generation in the north and perhaps two in the south. Polyphagous.	Green with whitish warts. Head brownish green and shield yellowish.
LEAF	Winged aphids are seen on leaf undersides in May. Colonies grow and trails of wax and honeydew accumulate. Severe browning of the foliage and blackening with sooty moulds follow, together with some leaf distortion.	Pale yellow-green aphid with faint transverse bands.
LEAF & SHOOT	Nymphs feed on leaves and shoots causing them to curl and shoots to distort, together forming a rosette-like growth covered in sooty moulds growing on the honeydew. Is a serious check to growth and can cause die-back.	Shiny blackish brown.
LEAF & SHOOT	At first green, later red 'currants' containing a single larva on leaves, petioles and young shoots inhibiting growth and producing a bushy top to oak stock. The alternate stage of the Common spangle gall to be found on the leaves of older trees (see p.37).	Small curved gall wasp larva.
NEEDLE LEAF & SHOOT	Very similar in habits to following species. Has predelction for larch but is a pronounced polyphage.	Covered in ashy-brown scales with black line between tops of wing covers. 4mm.
NEEDLE LEAF & SHOOT	Adult feeds on both broadleaved and coniferous species but is a pest on the latter. Removes triangular chunks from needle sides and browses on fine twig wood, ring-barking young plants. Has predelction for *Tsuga*. Larvae feed on fine roots of usually herbaceous weeds. Adult flightless.	A clay-coloured weevil. 5–7mm.

TIME OF DAMAGE	STAGE	ORDER AND FAMILY	LATIN NAME	ENGLISH NAME	TYPE OF CROP	DAMAGE RATING (see key p.12)	REFER-ENCE
May to Aug.	NYMPH & ADULT	COLLEMBOLA Sminthuridae	*Bourletiella hortensis* Plate 14	Garden spring-tail	Seedlings	XXXXX	28
Larva – April/May June/July	LARVA	LEPIDOPTERA Tortricidae	*Argyrotaenia pulchellana*	Grey red-barred tortrix	Seedlings	XX	118
May to July peak	NYMPH & ADULT	HEMIPTERA Callaphididae	*Phyllaphis fagi* Plate 58	Beech woolly aphid	All stock	XXXX	52
April to June/July	NYMPH & ADULT	HEMIPTERA Aphididae	*Myzus cerasi*	Cherry blackfly	All stock & older	XXXX	38
April to June	LARVA	HYMENOPTERA Cynipidae	*Neuroterus quercus-baccarum* Plate 49	Currant gall wasp	All stock & older	XXXX	7 71
April/May to Sept./Oct.	ADULT	COLEOPTERA Curculionidae	*Strophosomus melanogrammus* Plate 69	Nut leaf weevil	All stock	XXX	117
April to Oct.	ADULTS	COLEOPTERA Curculionidae	*Otiorhynchus singularis* Plate 52	Clay-coloured weevil	All stock	XXXX	117

PART OF TREE	DESCRIPTION OF DAMAGE AND FEEDING HABIT	DESCRIPTION OF DAMAGING STAGE *(see note on p.12)*
ROOT COLLAR	Adults ring-bark the stems of young seedlings. Damage somewhat similar to young cutworm. Polyphagous. Feeds at night.	(1) Small black weevil. 2–3mm. (2) Similar but with long black hairs.
ROOT COLLAR	Small larvae girdle seedlings, later chew through stem at ground level and pull the cut stem some way down into the soil. Feed at night.	(1) Dirty grey vaguely striped brownish or greenish. 30mm. (2) Brownish larva with dark brownish pear-shaped back marks. Yellowish stripe on sides. 30mm. (3) Brownish sometimes tinged greenish with yellow-brown back line, brownish lines bordered with a black dash on segments. 35mm.
ROOT	Young larvae prune roots and later sever them below ground level. Wilt of the top noticeable well after the damage is done. Adults feed on the leaves of broadleaved trees. *M. melolontha* is typical of heavy soils in the south; *S. brunnea* is most commonly the damaging species in Scotland. *P. horticola* prefers sandy soils and dunes.	Characteristically strongly curved larvae with swollen hind ends. Head brown. (1) 30mm. Adult brown. Head black. 30mm. (2) 15mm. Adult brown. 8–10mm. (3) 18mm. Adult brown. Head green. 6–8mm.
ROOT	Larvae prune roots of nursery stock and kill plants. Polyphagous.	Black weevil. 5mm.
ROOT	Kills stock through ring-barking below ground. Typically in highly organic soils where large dressings of peat or hop waste have been applied. (St Mark's Day is 25th May.)	Whitish-grey, long, midge larva with well-developed sclerotised head. Body with short spines.
ROOT	Larva eats out a deep spiral, ring-barking groove or completely severs main root.	Cream larva with horny brownish spots each with a short stiff hair. Head orange-brown. 35mm.
ROOT	Perhaps one of a number of nematode species which can reach pest status in forest nurseries. Causes patches of off-colour seedlings to appear in beds about June onwards. Growth ceases, infection spreads rapidly and is often a recurring trouble. Roots will be found to be 'stumpy', abbreviated and with dying tissue at tip. Occasionally large aggregations of nematodes are visible by ×15 lens.	Microscopical, worm-like, sharp at both ends.

TIME OF DAMAGE	STAGE	ORDER AND FAMILY	LATIN NAME	ENGLISH NAME	TYPE OF CROP	DAMAGE RATING *(see key p.12)*	REFER-ENCE
May to June	ADULT	COLEOPTERA Curculionidae	(1) *Barypeithes araneiformis* (2) *B. pellucidus* Plate 13	Strawberry fruit weevil Short snouted weevil	All stock	XXXXX	109 117
June to Sept./Oct. July to May July/Aug. to May	LARVAE	LEPIDOPTERA Noctuidae	(1) *Agrotis segetum* (2) *A. exclamationis* (3) *Noctua pronuba* Plate 6	Turnip moth Heart and dart moth Yellow underwing moth	All stock	XXXX XXXX XXX	2
Adults May to June Adults May to June Adults May to June	LARVAE	COLEOPTERA Scarabaidae	(1) *Melolontha melolontha* (2) *Serica brunnea* (3) *Phyllopertha horticola*	Cockchafer Brown chafer Garden chafer	All stock	XXXX XXXX XXXX	65
May/June peak	LARVA	COLEOPTERA Curculionidae	*Otiorhynchus ovatus*	Strawberry root weevil	All stock	XXXXX	117
Spring & summer	LARVA	DIPTERA Bibionidae	*Bibio* spp.	St Mark's fly and others	All stock	XXXX	119
Aug. to April Adult May to July	LARVA	LEPIDOPTERA Hepialidae	*Hepialus humuli* Plate 37	Ghost swift moth	All stock and older	XXXX	65
May to Sept.	ADULT & LARVA	Nematoda	*Dolichorhynchus microphasmis* Plate 29		Seedlings	XXXXX	

PART OF TREE	DESCRIPTION OF DAMAGE AND FEEDING HABIT	DESCRIPTION OF DAMAGING STAGE *(see note on p.12)*

UNDER GLASS

NEEDLE	An occasional pest of conifers under glass. Causes yellowing of foliage and reduction of growth.	Shining yellow-green with very distinct black horseshoe mark on back.
NEEDLE	Needles turn dingy yellow with a great deal of silk strung across all parts of crown. Minute red eggs massed on young wood. Mites on needles.	Minute, opalescent, pale yellowish green spinning mite.
LEAF	A number of whitefly species feed on broadleaved trees occasionally become pest under protected cultivation particularly where large plants are being raised and may have an extended greenhouse life. New growth is attacked. Female usually lays eggs in circles or arcs. Feeding of nymphs produces great quantities of honeydew on which a felt of mould grows. Distortion, reduction in growth and discolouration result.	Small white, very active, aphid-like. Winged adult appearing to jump when disturbed. Immature stages sedentary.
ROOT	Damage to all species may occur if grown in peaty media. Feeding on conifers is upon root hairs and fine roots causing wilt and death. On broadleaves feeding may also be on cotyledons before their emergence above ground.	Slender midge larvae often with black heads.
ROOT & NEEDLE	Larvae feed on fine roots of a wide range of tree seedlings grown in peaty composts. Adults chew leaves at night.	Larva a typical weevil, curved yellowish white and wrinkled. Head brown. 12mm. Adult black with longitudinal lines of yellow scaly hairs. 9–10mm.

TIME OF DAMAGE	STAGE	ORDER AND FAMILY	LATIN NAME	ENGLISH NAME	TYPE OF CROP	DAMAGE RATING *(see key p.12)*	REFER-ENCE
All year round	NYMPH & ADULT	HEMIPTERA Aphididae	*Aulacorthum circumflexum*	Mottled arum aphid	Conifer seedlings	XXX	
May to Sept.	MITE	ACARI Tetranychidae	*Oligonychus ununguis* Plate 50	Conifer spinning mite	All conifers	XXXX	82
Spring & summer	NYMPH & ADULT	HEMIPTERA Aleyrodidae	Aleyrodid spp.	Whitefly	Broad-leaved	XXX	96
All year round	LARVA	DIPTERA Mycetophilidae	Sciarid spp.	Fungus gnats	Seedlings	XXXXX	96
All year round	ADULT & LARVA	COLEOPTERA Curculionidae	*Otiorhynchus sulcatus*	Black vine or Cyclamen weevil	Seedlings	XXXXX	96

PART OF TREE	DESCRIPTION OF DAMAGE AND FEEDING HABIT	DESCRIPTION OF DAMAGING STAGE (see note on p.12)

CONIFERS (GENERAL)

NEEDLE	Needles turn dingy yellow. A great deal of silk thread strung across all parts of crown. Minute red eggs massed on young wood. Mites on needles.	Minute, opalescent, pale yellowish green spinning mite.
NEEDLE	Feeds on inner side of needles at shoot tips in spun needles. Damage to shoot causes distortion.	Dark green to greenish black, side line paler. Head light brown marked with black. 10–12mm.
NEEDLE & BUD	Mines into leaves and buds causing shoot dieback and multi-leaders. Common where cultivation removes the normal heathland food plants.	Pale greenish-yellow with central and side stripes, bold, broad olive-green. Head and shield pale brown. 12–15mm.
NEEDLE	Two from a large genus of leaf feeding weevils, commoner perhaps on broadleaves but frequently damaging to conifers. Larvae feed on roots of a wide range of herbaceous and woody plants.	(1) Black with greenish-gold scales. 5–8mm. (2) Bright green or golden yellow. 3–6mm.
YOUNG STEM	Adult feeds on and ring-barks young transplants at lower stem levels (also feeds on crown branchwood, brambles and even broadleaved species). Breeds in stumps of felled conifers.	Large black weevil with diffusely transverse pattern of yellow scales. 9–13mm. Larva a wrinkled, curved whitish weevil with yellow-brown head. 15mm.
NEEDLE & SHOOT	Adult feeds on both broadleaved and coniferous species. Removes triangular chunks from needles and ring-barks young twigs. Can damage like *Hylobius*. Partial to *Tsuga*. Larvae feed on the roots of usually herbaceous weeds.	A clay-coloured weevil. 5–7mm.
NEEDLE & SHOOT	Very similar in habits to the above species. Has a predeliction for larch.	Covered in ashy-brown scales with black line between tops of wing covers. 4mm.
CONE	Distorts cone through feeding of larvae on scales and axis of cone. Much frass but little resin ejected. Also can bore down shoots causing them to crook and die.	Greenish background with longitudinal stripes of reddish-brown. 20–25mm.

TIME OF DAMAGE	STAGE	ORDER AND FAMILY	LATIN NAME	ENGLISH NAME	TYPE OF CROP	DAMAGE RATING *(see key p.12)*	REFER-ENCE
May to Sept.	MITE	ACARI Eriophyidae	*Oligonychus ununguis* Plate 50	Conifer spinning mite	All ages	XX	82 116
April/May to June	LARVA	LEPIDOPTERA Tortricidae	*Aphelia viburnana*	Bilberry tortrix	Young trees	XXX	42
July/Aug.	LARVA	LEPIDOPTERA Tortricidae	*Clepsis senecionana*	Rustic tortrix	Young trees	XXX	42
April to July	ADULTS	COLEOPTERA Curculionidae	(1) *Phyllobius pyri* (2) *P. argentatus*	Common leaf weevil	All ages	XX	117
All year round. Peaks May/ June & Aug.	ADULT	COLEOPTERA Curculionidae	*Hylobius abietis* Plate 39 See also p.135	Pine weevil	Trans-plants	XXXXX	104 121
April to Oct.	ADULT	COLEOPTERA Curculionidae	*Otiorhynchus singularis* Plate 52 See also p.136	Clay-coloured weevil	All ages	XXXXX	117
April/May to Sept./Oct.	ADULT	COLEOPTERA Curculionidae	*Strophosomus melanogrammus* Plate 69	Nut-leaved weevil	All ages	XXX	117
Aug. to May	LARVA	LEPIDOPTERA Pyralidae	*Dioryctria abietella* Plate 27	Pine knothorn moth	Cone-bearing	XXX	

PART OF TREE	DESCRIPTION OF DAMAGE AND FEEDING HABIT	DESCRIPTION OF DAMAGING STAGE *(see note on p.12)*
STEM & WOOD	Larvae bore tunnels at first shallowly and later deeply into the wood, packing frass behind them. They feed for up to 3 years in trees under stress, e.g. through old age, root rot under-thinning, and also in fresh-felled logs. Adults are large conspicuous insects either banded in black and yellow or shiny, steely-blue. The adults vector a 'wet rot' fungus which induces a vascular wilt of attacked live trees. Adult emergence holes round (oval in Longhorn beetles).	The larva is yellowish white with head brownish, very short stumpy legs, pronouncedly segmented with terminal spine. 20–30mm.
STEM & WOOD	Larvae bore in the cambial region of dead trees and waney-edged softwood timber. They make short irregular borings in both bark and wood and can be mistaken for bark beetles.	Larva whitish, curved, with legs. Adult reddish-brown, moderately hairy. 3–6mm.
WOOD	Gallery system blackened, 2, 3 or 4-branched bored into the wood. Initial entry is radial and proceeds in a circumferential direction; finally the egg niches are cut vertically. Small piles of white frass are diagnostic. An important technical pest of softwoods.	Black. Wing-covers black with yellow stripes. 3mm.
WOOD	Larva bores wandering tunnels of increasing diameter into wood, mainly in a radial direction. Tunnels are discoloured with fungus introduced by the female. Ejects huge quantities of frass. Tunnels in broadleaved trees cross-connected, scribing the wood at cambium level. Two year cycle.	Cream larva with sword-like process at tail. Hump behind head. 6–18mm. Adult long, slender yellow-brown to dark brown. 6–18mm.
WOOD	Larva in recently dead, felled or fire-damaged trees or stumps. Bores deep into the wood.	Larva a longhorn up to 20mm. Adult elongate, wing-covers with up to six raised lines on each. 10–16mm.
WOOD	The first to arrive after a fire. Also attacks decaying trees and stumps. Larva bores deep into the wood.	Larva a longhorn up to 34mm. Adult black-brown, wing covers with raised lines on each. 14–25mm.
WOOD	Larva bores between bark and cambium for up to 3 years. Pupates in a tunnel in the wood. A recognised pest of posts, palings and rustic work.	Larva a longhorn up to 24mm. Adult broad, flattish and dark purplish. 8–16mm.

TIME OF DAMAGE	STAGE	ORDER AND FAMILY	LATIN NAME	ENGLISH NAME	TYPE OF CROP	DAMAGE RATING (see key p.12)	REFER-ENCE
All year round. Adults June to Oct.	LARVAE	HYMENOPTERA Siricidae	*Urocerus gigas* *Sirex cyaneus* *Sirex juvencus*	Woodwasps	Pole to older	XX	4 119
Spring/ summer	LARVA	COLEOPTERA Anobiidae	*Ernobius mollis*	False furniture beetle	Pole & older	X	40
April to June/July	ADULT & LARVA	COLEOPTERA Scolytidae	*Xyloterus lineatus* Plate 73 & 97 See also p.125	Conifer ambrosia beetle	Logs & broken stems	XXXXX	27 39
June/July	LARVA	COLEOPTERA Lymexelidae	*Hylecoetus dermestoides* Plate 40	Large timberworm	Logs & stumps	XXX	39 40
Adult July/ Aug.	LARVA	COLEOPTERA Cerambycidae	*Asemum striatum*	Pine longhorn beetle	Wood	X	75
Adult June/ July	LARVA	COLEOPTERA Cerambycidae	*Arhopalus tristis* (*Criocephalus ferus*) Plate 11		Wood	X	75
Adult May/ June	LARVA	COLEOPTERA Cerambycidae	*Callidium violaceum*	Violet tanbark beetle	Cambium	X	75

PART OF TREE	DESCRIPTION OF DAMAGE AND FEEDING HABIT	DESCRIPTION OF DAMAGING STAGE *(see note on p.12)*

ABIES (SILVER FIR)

NEEDLE	First signs of attack are collections of wrinkled, twisted needles on current shoots. In severe attacks these wilt and drop and the shoot dies back. Attack is persistent, growth is inhibited and the crown reduces. A serious pest of *A. alba*, *A. cilcia* and *A. nordmanniana*. Can alternate on *Picea orientalis* only, on which small 'pineapple galls' develop and terminate the lateral shoots.	Blackish aphid with a fringe of wax; in large colonies. Much honeydew.
NEEDLE & SHOOT	Causes development of 'gouty' swellings on shoots, termination of growth and finally death of plants. These are the symptoms on *A. nordmanniana*, *A. alba* and *A. balsamea*. On *A. grandis*, *A. lasciocarpa*, *A. procera* and *A. concolor* the species mainly infests stems which results in 'rotholz', a type of pressure wood. No alternate host.	Dirty grey aphid in fluffy waxy wool.
NEEDLE	On expanding shoots, in colonies, feeding on the needles, causing them to twist at the shoot tip. Damaged needles are retained.	Small very pale aphid covered in fluffy wax.
SEED	Eats out the contents of seed. On emergence leaves small round hole. Can account for a high proportion of seed particularly in an otherwise poor seed year.	Larva a small gall wasp. 2mm. Adult black sometimes marked with yellow.
STEM	Egg gallery irregular, rather wide, often hooked. In felled or dead trees; galleries often mixed with those of *Hylurgops palliatus*.	Brown to dark brown beetle clothed in longish yellow hair. 3.5–4mm.

CEDRUS (CEDAR)

SHOOT	Feeds between scales of dwarf shoots, causes loss of older needles and die-back of twigs and branches. Much honeydew.	Very small light brown aphid. Up to 1.5mm.

JUNIPERUS (JUNIPER)

NEEDLE	Mines needles and webs foliage causing die-back of branches.	Body grey with brownish sides. Three reddish brown stripes. Head and shield reddish-brown.

TIME OF DAMAGE	STAGE	ORDER AND FAMILY	LATIN NAME	ENGLISH NAME	TYPE OF CROP	DAMAGE RATING (see key p.12)	REFER-ENCE
May through summer	NYMPH & ADULT	HEMIPTERA Adelgidae	*Adelges nordmannianae* Plate 5	Silver fir woolly aphid	All ages	XXXXX	50
All year round	NYMPH & ADULT	HEMIPTERA Adelgidae	*Adelges piceae*	Balsam woolly aphid	All ages	XXXXX	50
June	ADULT & LARVA	HEMIPTERA Thelaxidae	*Mindarus abietinus*	Balsam twig aphid	Young trees	XX	58
July to May	LARVA	HYMENOPTERA Torymidae	*Megastigmus pinus*	Silver fir seed wasp	Seed bearers	XXXXX	119
May to July	LARVA	COLEOPTERA Scolytidae	*Dryocoetes autographus* Plate 78	Silver fir bark beetle	Pole to older	s	117

TIME OF DAMAGE	STAGE	ORDER AND FAMILY	LATIN NAME	ENGLISH NAME	TYPE OF CROP	DAMAGE RATING	REFER-ENCE
May	NYMPH & ADULT	HEMIPTERA Lachnidae	*Cedrobium lapportei*		All ages	XXXX	55

TIME OF DAMAGE	STAGE	ORDER AND FAMILY	LATIN NAME	ENGLISH NAME	TYPE OF CROP	DAMAGE RATING	REFER-ENCE
May to June	LARVA	LEPIDOPTERA Gelechiidae	*Dichomeris marginella*	Juniper webber moth	All ages	XXX	

PART OF TREE	DESCRIPTION OF DAMAGE AND FEEDING HABIT	DESCRIPTION OF DAMAGING STAGE *(see note on p.12)*

LARIX (LARCH)

NEEDLE	The most damaging adelgid species on larch. Often numerous, feeding on needles which turn brown. Causes severe needle loss and shoot die-back. Produces copious honeydew. Alternates on *Picea*.	Small purple grey aphid, naked at first, later covered in blue-white wax.
NEEDLE	The earliest adelgid on larch. Produces a characteristic elbowed kink on needles of the dwarf shoots and epicormic needles. Alternates on spruces making usually single pineapple-shaped galls often marked with semicircular, deep pink lines of hairs, opening in June/July.	Small greenish aphid with little wool.
NEEDLE	Feeds on needles within silken pipes, causing browning and needle loss. Can completely defoliate; trees then become dressed in silk. Repeated defoliation can contribute to tree death.	Yellow-grey larva when young, later grey with purple stripe and finally all reddish purple. 11mm.
NEEDLE	Larvae feed on needles of dwarf shoots; damaged remnants turn brown becoming obvious about August. Prefers Japanese and Hybrid larch (compare *Coleophora laricella* below).	Green larva with dark stripes. 'Humped' appearance. Head light brown. 10–14mm.
NEEDLE	Feeds on long and dwarf shoots.	Green larva with dark stripes. Head green with some brown markings. 10–12mm.
NEEDLE	Feeds on opening buds and long shoots. Causes browning of patches of trees particularly on edges.	Olive to grass green larva. Head yellow-brown. 12–16mm.
NEEDLE	Feeds mostly on dwarf shoots and can cause patchy browning. Prefers European larch. Two generations a year.	Green larva with four white stripes. Head yellow speckled brown. 10–14mm.
NEEDLE	Feed at first as a clutch, later independently. Egg-laying into slit made into lower surface of long shoot which causes it to curl down characteristically. A serious pest at beginning of 20th century, killing trees.	Large dirty cream larva with grey stripe down back; a white 'collar' and black head. 21mm.
NEEDLE & SHOOT	Larvae spin new shoots together and feed within webbing tubes, eating needles from tip. Needles turn reddish-brown and shoots may die back causing crown distortions.	Usually more or less uniformly black to greyish black (contrast with forms on pine and spruce). 9–10mm.

TIME OF DAMAGE	STAGE	ORDER AND FAMILY	LATIN NAME	ENGLISH NAME	TYPE OF CROP	DAMAGE RATING *(see key p.12)*	REFER-ENCE
May to Sept.	NYMPH & ADULT	HEMIPTERA Adelgidae	*Adelges laricis* Plate 4	Larch woolly aphid	All ages	XXXX	50
May to June	NYMPH & ADULT	HEMIPTERA Adelgidae	*Adelges viridis*		All ages	X	50
June/July	LARVA	HYMENOPTERA Pamphiliidae	*Cephalcia lariciphila* Plate 18 See also p.131	Web-spinning larch sawfly	Pole & older	XXXX	35 37 105 115
June/Oct.	LARVA	HYMENOPTERA Tenthredinidae	*Anoplonyx destructor* Plate 9	Benson's larch sawfly	Pole & older	XXX	67
May/June	LARVA	HYMENOPTERA Tenthredinidae	*Pachynematus imperfectus* Plate 53	Larch sawfly	Pole	X	119
June/early July	LARVA	HYMENOPTERA Tenthredinidae	*Pristiphora wesmaeli* Plate 63	Larch sawfly	Thicket	XXX	119
May to Sept.	LARVA	HYMENOPTERA Tenthredinidae	*Pristiphora laricis*	Small larch sawfly	Thicket & pole	XX	119
June to July	LARVA	HYMENOPTERA Tenthredinidae	*Pristiphora erichsonii*	Large larch sawfly	Pole & older	XXXXX	119
May to July	LARVA	LEPIDOPTERA Tortricidae	*Zeiraphera diniana* Plate 74 See also p.130	Larch bud moth	All ages	XXXX	20 43 73

PART OF TREE	DESCRIPTION OF DAMAGE AND FEEDING HABIT	DESCRIPTION OF DAMAGING STAGE *(see note on p.12)*
NEEDLE	Mines needles and travels in a 'case' or tube of emptied needles. Damaged foliage at first appears whitish, turning through yellow to brown. Superficially like *A. destructor* damage but earlier, in late May/June. Often confused with frost damage. Overwinters at base of dwarf shoots and beneath bark scales of branch and stem wood.	Larva brownish-red. Head black. 5mm.
CONE	Attack made at pollination time. Larva feeds on seed and cone parts. Cone weeps resin and frass is ejected. Cone distorts.	Yellowish-white larva. 6–7mm.
SHOOT	Bores up the current year's shoot causing it to lose needles and to die. Small round hole at base of dead shoot marks emergence (ragged hole indicates bird predation).	Larva pale yellow at first, later reddish-grey with a darker stripe at hind end. Head is black. 5–7mm.
STEM & BRANCH	Aphid secretes wax and feeds in fissures of young tissue where it forms lines on undersides of branches. In winter found in branch and stem crevices often causing exfoliation of bark flakes.	Oval yellow-green aphid with milky-blue wax and honeydew.
STEM	Egg gallery extensive, typically 3-armed, star-shaped. Maturation feeding by adult in up to 4-year-old shoots of larch; these break off at the point of injury. A very aggressive bark beetle which can carry an aggressive wilt fungus. A northerly species in UK so far.	Blackish bark beetle with pronounced excavation at hind end, toothed and dull matt. 5–6mm.
WOOD	Normally in stumps where its oval emergence holes are very common. Will attack green trees when droughted, suffering from root fungus attack or otherwise debilitated.	Cream coloured larva deeply segmented. Head light brown. 8–17mm.

PICEA (SPRUCE)

NEEDLE	Feeds on undersides of needles causing yellowing and loss of old needles. Defoliation of N. American spruces normally worse than those from Eurasia.	Small green, active aphid with red eyes. 1.5mm.
NEEDLE	Needles turn dingy yellow. A great deal of silk thread strung across all parts of crown. Minute red eggs massed on young wood. Mites on needles.	Minute, opalescent, pale yellowish-green spinning mite.
NEEDLE	Needles turn reddish. Silk as above species. Eggs on needles. Damage proceeds from inside crown outwards.	Minute pale yellow elongate mite.

TIME OF DAMAGE	STAGE	ORDER AND FAMILY	LATIN NAME	ENGLISH NAME	TYPE OF CROP	DAMAGE RATING *(see key p.12)*	REFER-ENCE
July to May	LARVA	LEPIDOPTERA Coleophoridae	*Coleophora laricella* Plate 20	Larch casebearer	Thicket & later	XXX	65
June to July	LARVA	DIPTERA Anthomyiidae	*Lasiomma melania*	Larch cone fly	Cone bearers	XX	119
June to April	LARVA	LEPIDOPTERA Yponomeutidae	*Argyresthia laevigatella*	Larch shoot moth	Thicket	XX	65
All year round	NYMPH & ADULT	HEMIPTERA Adelgidae	*Adelges viridana*		Pole	X	49 50
Peaks May/ June & Aug/Sept.	ADULT & LARVA	COLEOPTERA Scolytidae	*Ips cembrae* Plates 41 and 83 See also p.123	Large larch bark beetle	Pole to older	s or XXXXX	133 131
July to Oct.	LARVA	COLEOPTERA Cerambycidae	*Tetropium gabrieli* Plate 71	Larch longhorn beetle	Pole to older	XXX	125

Sept./June	NYMPH & ADULT	HEMIPTERA Aphididae	*Elatobium abietinum* Plate 31 See also pp.134 & 138	Green spruce aphid	All ages	XXXX	51
May to Sept.	MITE	ACARI Tetranychidae	*Oligonychus ununguis* Plate 50 See also p.137	Conifer spinning mite	All ages	XX	82 116
Autumn to spring	MITE	ACARI Eriophyidae	*Nalepella haarlovi*		Thicket	X	116

PART OF TREE	DESCRIPTION OF DAMAGE AND FEEDING HABIT	DESCRIPTION OF DAMAGING STAGE *(see note on p.12)*
SHOOT & NEEDLE	Feeds on developing shoot tips and needles causing brown patches and bent, twisted needles which persist.	Small very pale yellowish aphid covered in fluffy wax.
NEEDLE	Prefers older needles of the top three or four whorls. Young larvae eat out pieces, older ones the whole needle. Sitka spruce tops turn yellowish whilst Norway spruce a red-brown. Can cause die-back of branches and crown distortions, particularly in Norway spruce.	Dark green larva with five white stripes. 15mm.
NEEDLE	Feeds as a clutch on the current year's shoots as they flush. Prefers the top of the crown. Causes shoot die-back and crown distortions.	All green larva with yellowish head. 10–15mm.
NEEDLE	When young feeds on current year's growth and moves to older needles later.	Browny-green with three dark green/olive stripes. Head grass green with darker patterning. 12–15mm.
NEEDLE	Typically seen only on the top few whorls of tall *P. abies*. Causes very obvious browning, some die-back of shoots and crown distortions. Common in Scotland and Border country.	Light green, black-spotted larva. Head brown-yellow flecked with dark brown at back. 10mm.
NEEDLE	Young larvae feed on new needles and later on older ones. Short feeding period.	Green larva with five darker stripes. Head greenish with dark 'eyebrows'. 14–17mm.
NEEDLE	Tassel similar to that of *Zeiraphera ratzburgiana* but shorter and bud scales not spun to tip. Mines a few needles only and removes bud, terminating shoot. Very short feeding period. Damage often confused with frost.	Small greenish-white. Head yellow-brown. 7mm.
NEEDLE	Mines into needles and buds causing die-back and multi-leaders. Common when cultivation removes normal heathland food-plants. Overwinters as a larva in a silk shelter.	Pale greenish yellow larva with central and side stripes bold, broad, olive green. Head and neck pale brown. 12–15mm.
NEEDLE	Mines needles and spins them together itself moving in a silken tube. Common on lower branches.	Small dirty greenish larva.
NEEDLE	Mines needles and spins them together in fan-shaped bundles with frass and remains. Damaging on young plants and Christmas trees. Pupates in spring in litter.	Green to yellow with red-brown lines down back. Brown head and neck shield. 9mm.

TIME OF DAMAGE	STAGE	ORDER AND FAMILY	LATIN NAME	ENGLISH NAME	TYPE OF CROP	DAMAGE RATING *(see key p.12)*	REFER-ENCE
July	NYMPH & ADULT	HEMIPTERA Thelaxidae	*Mindarus obliquus*	Spruce twig aphid	Young trees	X	58
June/Sept.	LARVA	HYMENOPTERA Diprionidae	*Gilpinia hercyniae* Plate 35 See also p.132	European spruce sawfly	Thicket & over	XXX	34 1 36 77
May/June	LARVA	HYMENOPTERA Tenthredinidae	*Pristiphora abietina* Plate 62 See also p.138	Gregarious spruce sawfly	All ages	XX	119
May/July	LARVA	HYMENOPTERA Tenthredinidae	*Pristiphora saxesenii*		Pole & older	XX	119
June/July	LARVA	HYMENOPTERA Tenthredinidae	*Pristiphora subarctica*	Scandinavian spruce sawfly	Pole & older	XX	119
June	LARVA	HYMENOPTERA Tenthredinidae	*Pachynematus scutellatus*		All ages	XX	119
May/June	LARVA	HYMENOPTERA Tenthredinidae	*Pristiphora ambigua*	Spruce tip sawfly	Thicket	X	65
July/Aug. to April	LARVA	LEPIDOPTERA Tortricidae	*Clepsis senecionana*	Rustic tortrix	Trans-plants	XX	42
Sept./May	LARVA	LEPIDOPTERA Tortricidae	*Epinotia nanana*	Dwarf spruce bell moth	All ages	XXX	93 118
Aug./Dec.	LARVA	LEPIDOPTERA Tortricidae	*Epinotia tedella* Plate 32 See also p.138	Spruce bell moth	All ages	XXX	118

PICEA (SPRUCE)

PART OF TREE	DESCRIPTION OF DAMAGE AND FEEDING HABIT	DESCRIPTION OF DAMAGING STAGE *(see note on p.12)*
NEEDLE & SHOOT	Larvae spin new shoots together and feed within webbing tubes, eating needles from tip. Needles turn reddish-brown and shoots may die back causing crown distortions.	Body grey with black dots; very variable. Head black. 9–10mm.
NEEDLE	Grazes needle ends and lower side of flushing shoot stem, causing a brown, curved, short-lived tassel with bud scales spun to tassel tip. Tassel needles fall and damage terminates shoot. Egg overwinters. Also feeds on spruce flowers.	Whitish grey larva with brown head. 8mm.
NEEDLE	Larvae eat only a part of each needle down from the tip giving a bottle-brush appearance to affected trees. The cut needle ends turn brown. Virus disease of larvae can cause collapse of population. Defoliation can result in tree deaths. Outbreaks typically on heather-covered ridges.	Greyish to grey-black larva with two black hair pencils on side of head and a brownish one on tail. Four yellow 'shaving brushes' down back as well as fine orange and white lines.
BUD & NEEDLE	Mite feeding kills buds. Dormant buds do not take over and resulting growth is characteristically 'snakey'. Mites in masses under bark scales.	Minute, elongate, light yellow mite.
SHOOT	Damage to spruce more or less confined to the galls and to kinking or termination of the shoot (but see *A. abietis* below). Can be separated when fresh in June as follows: 1½ times or more longer than wide .... *A. cooleyi.* (migrates to *Pseudotsuga*) Roughly spherical yellow/greenish gall on weak side-shoots .... *A. laricis.* (migrates to *Larix*) Pineapple-shaped with deep pink, semicircular lines of hairs: occurring singly, opening June/July .... *A. viridis.* (migrates to *Larix*) occurring in groups at base of vigorous shoots opening in Aug./Sept. .... *A. abietis* (See under 'Christmas trees')	Small dark near-purple nymphs. Winged adults darker.
SHOOT	A Christmas tree pest. Does not alternate to another conifer. Can build up high numbers on a single tree in successive seasons.	
YOUNG SHOOT	Colonies of aphids at bud-burst move to current year's shoots. Copious honeydew and sooty moulds. Shoots tend to snake or curl and needles wilt particularly on undersides of side shoots. A serious pest of Christmas trees.	Pale brown or pale grey-green with dense wax covering.

TIME OF DAMAGE	STAGE	ORDER AND FAMILY	LATIN NAME	ENGLISH NAME	TYPE OF CROP	DAMAGE RATING (see key p.12)	REFER-ENCE
May to July	LARVA	LEPIDOPTERA Tortricidae	Zeiraphera diniana Plate 74 See also p.130	Larch bud moth	All ages	XXXX	20 43 73
May/June	LARVA	LEPIDOPTERA Tortricidae	Zeiraphera ratzeburgiana	Spruce tip tortrix	Thicket	X	43 110 118
May to July/ Aug.	LARVA	LEPIDOPTERA Lymantriidae	Orgyia antiqua	Vapourer moth	All ages	XXXX	118
May/June/July	MITE	ACARI Eriophyidae	Trisetacus grosmanni	Sitka spruce bud mite	All ages	X	85
Summer	NYMPH	HEMIPTERA Adelgidae	Adelges spp. Plates 2, 3 and 4	Pineapple gall aphids	Mostly young	X	50
May/June	NYMPH	HEMIPTERA Adelgidae	Adelges abietis Plate 2 See also p.137	Pineapple gall woolly aphid	Young trees	XXX	50
May to July	NYMPH & ADULT	HEMIPTERA Lachnidae	Cinara pilicornis See also p.138	Brown spruce shoot aphid	Young trees	XX or XXXX	55

PART OF TREE	DESCRIPTION OF DAMAGE AND FEEDING HABIT	DESCRIPTION OF DAMAGING STAGE (see note on p.12)
NEEDLE, BUD & SHOOT	Young nymphs on buds and needle undersides of new shoots of outer crown.	Very small scale. Female oval reddish and larvae similar.
CONE	Feeds internally on axis and seeds of cone.	White or yellowish with pale brown hairs. Head and neck shield light brown.
SHOOT	Serious pest of Sitka spruce in British Columbia. Attack on year-old leaders. Larvae bore downwards. Needles turn red and shoot wilts, droops and falls off later. Symptoms in July. Minimum of 888 degree-days above 7.2°C necessary for development.	Pitchy red-brown weevil with white and yellow scales on wing-covers. 4–6mm.
STEM	Feeding of often enormous colonies on stem appear to have little effect on tree. Honeydew copious and often hinders forest operations.	Large black aphid with long legs.
STEM	Egg gallery usually 3–7 armed, star-shaped with centre brood chamber. Arms curve into star. Often found with *Ips typographus* and appears to accept smaller-sized material in weaker state.	Dark brown to reddish-brown. Excavation at tail with a few hairs, strongly toothed, glistening. 2–3.5mm.
STEM	Egg gallery with 3–4 arms entering brood chamber more directly and vertically than above species. Tends to infest upper third or so of trees particularly where lower stem contains *I. typographus*. Will only breed in vertical material.	Light to dark brown. Distinctly excavated and toothed at tail. 3–4mm.
STEM	Mostly 2-armed, often 3 and up to 7 vertical arms with central chamber. Arms of varying length. Maturation feeding within the brood system and also in 'bad weather' communal and separate ones. Associated with a wilt fungus and is probably Europe's most aggressive bark beetle.	Dark brown to blackish. Excavation at tail toothed and soapy matt. 4–5.5mm.
STEM	Egg gallery is vertical and plugged with resinous frass at its entrance. Larvae feed communally at first but later construct their own tunnel which interweaves with others. Overwinters in tree bases. No pitch-tubes. Builds up in slash and windblow. Very aggressive at high densities.	Dark brown to black with reddish wing-covers, hairy. 4–7mm.

TIME OF DAMAGE	STAGE	ORDER AND FAMILY	LATIN NAME	ENGLISH NAME	TYPE OF CROP	DAMAGE RATING (see key p.12)	REFER-ENCE
May and all year	NYMPH & ADULT	HEMIPTERA Coccidae	*Physokermes piceae*	Spruce whorl scale insect	Pole & older	X	116
Aug. to April	LARVA	LEPIDOPTERA Tortricidae	*Cydia strobilella*		Cone-bearing	XX	43 13
May to July	ADULT & LARVA	COLEOPTERA Curculionidae	*Pissodes strobi** Plate 61	White pine weevil	Thicket & older	XXXX*	107 124
April to Sept.	NYMPH & ADULT	HEMIPTERA Lachnidae	*Cinara piceae*	Great black spruce bark aphid	Pole	X	55
Spring & summer	LARVA	COLEOPTERA Scolytidae	*Ips amitinus**	Smaller 8-toothed spruce bark beetle	Pole & older	XXXXX*	117
Spring & summer	LARVA	COLEOPTERA Scolytidae	*Ips duplicatus**		Pole & older	XXXXX*	16 117
May to Sept.	LARVA	COLEOPTERA Scolytidae	*Ips typographus** Plates 42 and 84	8-toothed spruce bark beetle	Pole & older	XXXXX*	17 18 117
June to July Two year cycle	LARVA	COLEOPTERA Scolytidae	*Dendroctonus rufipennis* Plate 77	Spruce beetle	Pole & older	XXXXX*	44 155

PART OF TREE	DESCRIPTION OF DAMAGE AND FEEDING HABIT	DESCRIPTION OF DAMAGING STAGE *(see note on p.12)*
STEM	Egg gallery unique in Europe: a broad frass and resin-packed tube in which eggs are laid. Larvae feed as a clutch and excavate a very large chamber which is packed in characteristic way with islands of frass. Enormous flows of resin on stem and presence of pitch-tubes is diagnostic. Attacks are often single and occlusion of damage common. Seldom kills favoured host *P. abies* but often kills Sitka spruce after 2 or 3 years' successive attacks.	Large, uniformly dull dark brown. 6–8mm.
STEM & ROOT	Egg gallery vertical with a crotch brood chamber at base. Maturation feeding of adult upon root collar region of young transplants causing death. Breeding and feeding of larvae in stumps and main roots and on undersides of logs lying in contact with the ground. Distinguished from *H. ater* only with difficulty.	Black, parallel-sided. 3–5mm.
STEM	Egg gallery a 3-armed star in the inner bark region. Attack usually on root-rotten or droughted trees. A southern species in Britain.	Brownish black wing covers with dense yellow scales. 2–3mm.
YOUNG STEM OR TWIG	Egg gallery diminutive, star-shaped and three or more armed. Attacks green twigs up to 1cm diameter, often ring-barking and killing them.	Tiny dark red-brown beetle. 1–1.8mm.
STEM	Egg gallery irregular, rather wide, often hooked. In felled or dead trees. Galleries often in mixture with those of *Hylurgops palliatus*.	Brown to dark brown beetle clothed in longish yellow hair. 3.5–4mm.
STEM	Egg gallery star-shaped and 3–5-armed with central brood chamber. Maturation within gallery. Common small beetle attacking dead trees and small felling waste.	Dark brown to black with reddish brown wing covers. 1.5–2.5mm.
STEM	Egg gallery often within the bark and very diffuse. Sometimes star-shaped at first, later feeding communally in a chamber. Breeds and feeds in felled produce only. Is an efficient carrier of bluestain fungus.	Adult brown to dark brown, dull. Thorax broad and narrowing to front. 3–4mm.
STEM	Egg gallery a blackened 2, 3 or 4 branched system bored into the wood. Initial entry is radial and proceeds in a circumferential direction; finally the egg niches are cut vertically. Small piles of white frass are diagnostic. An important technical pest of softwoods.	Head black. Wing-covers black with yellow stripes. 3mm.

TIME OF DAMAGE	STAGE	ORDER AND FAMILY	LATIN NAME	ENGLISH NAME	TYPE OF CROP	DAMAGE RATING *(see key p.12)*	REFER-ENCE
July to Sept. One to two year cycle	LARVA	COLEOPTERA Scolytidae	*Dendroctonus micans* Plates 26 and 76 See also p.122	Great spruce bark beetle	Pole & older	XXX or XXXX	32 90
May/July to Aug./April overlapping	ADULT & LARVA	COLEOPTERA Scolytidae	*Hylastes cunicularius*	Black spruce beetle	Trans-plants	XXXXX	121
May to Sept.	LARVA	COLEOPTERA Scolytidae	*Polygraphus poligraphus* Plate 90	Small spruce bark beetle	Pole to older	XXX	103 117
May to July	LARVA	COLEOPTERA Scolytidae	*Pityophthorus pubescens* Plate 89	Pine twig bark beetle	Pole & older	X	117
May to July	LARVA	COLEOPTERA Scolytidae	*Dryocoetus autographus* Plate 78	Silver fir bark beetle	Pole & older	s	117
May to July	LARVA	COLEOPTERA Scolytidae	*Pityogenes bidentatus* Plate 87	Two-toothed pine beetle	All ages (thin bark parts)	XX	117
May to Sept.	LARVA	COLEOPTERA Scolytidae	*Hylurgops palliatus* Plate 81		Felled produce	X	117
April to June/July	ADULT & LARVA	COLEOPTERA Scolytidae	*Xyloterus lineatus* Plates 73 and 97 See also p.125	Conifer ambrosia beetle	Logs, broken stems	XXX	27 39

PART OF TREE	DESCRIPTION OF DAMAGE AND FEEDING HABIT	DESCRIPTION OF DAMAGING STAGE *(see note on p.12)*
ROOT	Feeds on the fine roots of standing trees. Colonies with plentiful waxy wool. Said to be associated with dry conditions. No damage obvious.	Cream-coloured aphid with wool.
WOOD	Larvae mine between the wood and bark of dead and dying trees, in all sizes of material. Pupate in a curved tunnel in the wood plugged with two wads of frass packed on each side of the pupa.	Larva a longhorn. 14mm. Adult. Wing covers foreshortened revealing the diaphanous underwings. The whole a reddish-brown to darker. 5–15mm.

PINUS (PINE)

NEEDLE	Feeds on *P. sylvestris* and *P. contorta* causing yellowing of foliage. A southern species.	Dark greenish with blackish markings.
NEEDLE	Feeds as a compact colony on the current year's needles of many pine species. Very common. Can cause yellowing of foliage.	Grey aphid covered in dirty grey wax.
NEEDLE	Fairly common on many pine species particularly *P. nigra*. Feeds on mostly old foliage and appears not to be damaging.	Elongate, orange-red, blue-grey or brownish with sometimes a tuft of mealy secretion at hind end. Active.
NEEDLE	Common on *P. sylvestris* and *P. nigra*, causing premature fall of older foliage.	Elongate, slim aphid. Bright green dotted in dark colour. Active if disturbed.
NEEDLE	Feeds singly on older needles and often found with following species *D. pini*. May be two generations a year.	Head black. Body with dark background and double black stripe down back, decorated with white dots and yellow oblique dashes and commas down side. 28mm.
NEEDLE	Feeds as a clutch. Chews needles of all ages down to base. Defoliates branches or whole trees.	Brown to black head. Cream body with black dots. 25mm.
NEEDLE	Feeds as a clutch. Chews needles of all but current year down to base leaving bare portions of branch behind current growth.	Head black. Dirty grey-green body with diffuse dark stripe down back. 23mm.
NEEDLE	Chews chunks out of needles. An untidy feeder, often leaving mid-rib only or bits of needles, often hanging in random webs of silk. A serious pest of *P. sylvestris* and *P. contorta* in UK.	Green 'looper' with white stripes extending down head and body. 26mm.

TIME OF DAMAGE	STAGE	ORDER AND FAMILY	LATIN NAME	ENGLISH NAME	TYPE OF CROP	DAMAGE RATING (see key p.12)	REFER-ENCE
All year	NYMPH & ADULT	HEMIPTERA Pemphigidae	*Pachypappa tremulae* Plate 54	Spruce root aphid	Thicket & pole	X	135
Adults Aug. to July	LARVA	COLEOPTERA Cerambycidae	*Molorchus minor*		Wood	X	75

May to Sept.	NYMPH & ADULT	HEMIPTERA Lachnidae	*Cinara pini*		All ages	X	55
Spring to summer	NYMPH & ADULT	HEMIPTERA Lachnidae	*Schizolachnus pineti*	Grey pine needle aphid	Young trees	XX	55
Summer to autumn	NYMPH & ADULT	HEMIPTERA Lachnidae	*Eulachnus bluncki*	Narrow brown pine aphid	All ages	X	55
Spring to autumn	NYMPH & ADULT	HEMIPTERA Lachnidae	*Eulachnus agilis*	Spotted pine aphid	Thicket & older	XX	55
June to Sept.	LARVA	HYMENOPTERA Diprionidae	*Diprion simile*		Pole & older	X	119
May to June & Aug. to Sept.	LARVA	HYMENOPTERA Diprionidae	*Diprion pini* Plate 28 See also p.133	Large pine sawfly	Thicket to older	XXX	4 119
May to June	LARVA	HYMENOPTERA Diprionidae	*Neodiprion sertifer* Plate 47 See also p.133	Fox-coloured sawfly	Thicket & younger	XXX	4 47 101 119
June to Oct.	LARVA	LEPIDOPTERA Geometridae	*Bupalus piniaria* Plate 16 See also pp.126–7	Pine looper moth	Pole & older	XXXXX	21 31 69

PART OF TREE	DESCRIPTION OF DAMAGE AND FEEDING HABIT	DESCRIPTION OF DAMAGING STAGE *(see note on p.12)*
NEEDLE	Young larvae feed on developing 'candles', later chew whole needle pairs down to the sheath leaving jagged remains. Only known as a pest of *P. contorta* in UK, elsewhere of *P. sylvestris*. Kills trees and crops after a single defoliation.	Red-brown head. Green larva with white stripes.
NEEDLE	Mines into needles at first and later into shoots with needles spun together with silk.	Head and shield black. Body reddish.
NEEDLE & SHOOT	Larvae spin new shoots together and feed within web. Gross distortions of crowns result from die-back of shoots. Affected crops take on a grey-brown appearance.	Body grey with black dots; very variable. Head black. 9–10mm.
BUD & NEEDLE	Feeds within sheath on inside face of current year's needles, causing quick wilt, disguising damage and making diagnosis difficult. Needle pairs fall and are caught in the crown, inverted, with needles splayed. Defoliation may be impressive but recovery is good.	Small orange larva.
NEEDLE	Attack is upon the flushing shoot when needle pairs are about 3–7mm long. Larva settles between and at base of pair and eats out a cavity. The pair fuse and a swelling or sometimes quite conspicuous gall develops. Needle growth ceases, the colour turns through yellow to brown and the pairs drop usually in winter. Probably more common in the north. One generation a year.	Small orange-red midge larva.
NEEDLE	Mines needles at first and later bores into needle base. Needle loss causes die-back of shoots.	Reddish-brown body and head. Shield darker.
NEEDLE	Larvae eat only a part of each needle down from the tip giving a bottle-brush appearance to affected trees. The cut needle ends turn brown. Defoliation can result in tree deaths. Outbreaks typically on heather-covered ridges.	Greyish to grey-black larva with two black hair pencils on side of head and a brownish one on tail. Four yellow 'shaving brushes' down back as well as fine orange and white lines.
NEEDLE	Bare patches on terminal parts of branches are diagnostic. Larva feeds within the unflushed bud either causing it to abort or to produce shortened needle pairs. More obvious is adult feeding on needle which shows as a small yellow dot with central hole, needle remaining green. Repeated heavy defoliation may be fatal.	Larva a small weevil. Adult red-brown with a black snout and grey, scaly thorax. 2–3mm.

TIME OF DAMAGE	STAGE	ORDER AND FAMILY	LATIN NAME	ENGLISH NAME	TYPE OF CROP	DAMAGE RATING *(see key p.12)*	REFER- ENCE
May to July	LARVA	LEPIDOPTERA Noctuidae	*Panolis flammea* Plate 55 See also p.128	Pine beauty moth	Young pole to older	XXXXX	130 33
Sept. to May	LARVA	LEPIDOPTERA Gelechiidae	*Exoteleia dodecella*		Pole & older	XX	118
May to July	LARVA	LEPIDOPTERA Tortricidae	*Zeiraphera diniana* Plate 74 See also p.130	Larch budmoth	All ages	XXXX	20 43 73
June	LARVA	DIPTERA Cecidomyiidae	*Contarinia baeri* Plate 21	Pine needle midge	Thicket	XX	22 119
May to Nov.	LARVA	DIPTERA Cecidomyiidae	*Thecodiplosis brachyntera*	Pine needle shortening midge	All ages	XXX	22 119
Sept. to June/July	LARVA	LEPIDOPTERA Tortricidae	*Clavigesta purdeyi*		Pole & older	XX	120
May to July/ Aug.	LARVA	LEPIDOPTERA Lymantriidae	*Orgyia antiqua*	Vapourer moth	All ages	XXXX	118
July to Sept.	ADULT & LARVA	COLEOPTERA Curculionidae	*Brachonyx pineti* Plate 15	Pine needle weevil	Young trees	XXX	12

PART OF TREE	DESCRIPTION OF DAMAGE AND FEEDING HABIT	DESCRIPTION OF DAMAGING STAGE *(see note on p.12)*
SHOOT	Feeds on the current year's shoots of *P. sylvestris*, *P. nigra* and *P. contorta*.	Dark brown to orange brown. Large and active.
SHOOT	Commonest damage is to buds and developing shoots which are mined and killed causing multiple leaders and later forked stems. Less common is that leading to the classical 'post-horn' stem distortion. This results from usually older larvae boring along one side of a developing leader; the shoot flops over, the undamaged side grows on and the shoot extends in an arc such that the growing point returns to the original axis of growth. The 'resin tents' arising from larval feeding are characteristic.	Head and shield black. Body dark purplish-brown. 9mm.
BUD	Larvae feed on buds causing them to abort. Often accompanies above species.	Head black. Light dirty brown, each segment girthed with two thin red lines. 9–10mm.
BUD & NEEDLE	Young larvae feed within the sheath of developing needle pair, later boring either into the bud which aborts, or into the growing shoot which dies leaving a characteristic reddish papery tip. A northern species.	Head and shield black. Body pinkish-brown. 9mm.
BUD	Feeds among bud whorls but not necessarily damaging them. Activity, however, generates a persistent, say 4cm, ball of resin. More northerly species.	Head and shield dark brown. Body yellow-brown with small darker warts.
CONE	Feeds in the cones (and leaders) of *P. sylvestris*. Adult emerges from 2mm round hole in cone scale.	Larva a weevil. Adult black with cream scales on wing covers. 5–7mm. Very like *P. notatus* below.
SEED	Feeds on seeds within the cone. Adult emerges from round hole in scale (jagged holes indicate predation by birds).	Head and shield brown. Body greenish-yellow.
STEM	Mines into green pruning wounds and into the thick bark of *P. ponderosa*, *P. nigra* and *P. sylvestris* at base of stem. Common associate of *Peridermium pini* cankers.	Head brown with darker markings, shield paler. Body yellow-white.
STEM & BRANCH	Very common aphid on branches and young stems of *P. sylvestris* and *P. contorta*. Causes yellowing of foliage and shoot die-back where conditions are adverse. Plentiful honeydew.	Grey aphid with plentiful waxy wool.

TIME OF DAMAGE	STAGE	ORDER AND FAMILY	LATIN NAME	ENGLISH NAME	TYPE OF CROP	DAMAGE RATING (see key p.12)	REFER- ENCE
March to Sept.	NYMPH & ADULT	HEMIPTERA Lachnidae	*Cinara pinea*	Large pine aphid	All ages	X	55
Sept. to June	LARVA	LEPIDOPTERA Tortricidae	*Rhyacionia buoliana* Plate 66 See also p.129	Pine shoot moth	Thicket	XXX	120
Aug. to March	LARVA	LEPIDOPTERA Tortricidae	*Blastesthia turionella*	Pine bud moth	Thicket	X	120
May to Aug.	LARVA	LEPIDOPTERA Tortricidae	*Rhyacionia logaea*	Elgin shoot moth	Young thicket	XXX	120 151 152
July to May (Two years)	LARVA	LEPIDOPTERA Tortricidae	*Petrova resinella*	Pine resin gall moth	Young thicket	X	120
May to Sept.	LARVA	COLEOPTERA Curculionidae	*Pissodes validirostris*	Pine cone weevil	Cone- bearers	X	29 142
July to March/April	LARVA	LEPIDOPTERA Tortricidae	*Cydia conicolana*	Pine cone moth	Cone- bearers	X	26 87 86
Sept. to April	LARVA	LEPIDOPTERA Tortricidae	*Cydia coniferana*	Pine resin moth	Pole & older	XX	43
All year round	NYMPH & ADULT	HEMIPTERA Adelgidae	*Pineus pini*	Pine woolly aphid	Young trees & branches	XXX	50

PART OF TREE	DESCRIPTION OF DAMAGE AND FEEDING HABIT	DESCRIPTION OF DAMAGING STAGE *(see note on p.12)*
BRANCH	Large aggregations of mites produce a swollen 'plumber's joint' gall on young branches which open to release mites and subsequently forms into a canker-like growth.	Transparent elongate mite.
STEM	Quite specific to 5-needled pines and often on *P. strobus*. Very conspicuous waxy wool on stems. No obvious host reaction but there may be a connection with the rust fungus *Cronartium ribicola*.	A small greyish aphid covered with wax.
STEM	Typically breeds in dying and freshly felled trash. Adult an aggressive feeder on young growth of pole and younger stock. Feeding punctures on stems an obvious sign. Attacks predispose lower, older parts to attack for breeding. Larval tunnels long and wandering, frass-packed.	Larva a weevil. 7–9mm. Adult dark pitchy brown with cream and whitish scales.
STEM	Very similar in habits to above species, tending to breed in older, thicker barked stems. Less common and more a northern species.	Larva as above. Adult black, flattish with yellow scales in transverse bands.
STEM & ROOT	Egg gallery straight with crotch-shaped brood chamber. Maturation feeding of adults upon root collar region of transplants both above and below ground, ring-barking and killing plants. Breeding in the stumps and undersides of logs in contact with ground. The species is more southerly whilst *H. brunneus* dominates in the north.	Adult a black, shiny, parallel-sided beetle. 4–5mm. *H. brunneus* is duller, less parallel and marginally shorter. Three smaller *Hylastes* species are rarer.
STEM	Egg gallery often within the bark and very diffuse. Sometimes star-shaped at first, later feeding communally in a chamber. Breeds and feeds in felled produce only. Is an efficient carrier of bluestain fungus.	Adult brown to dark brown, dull. Thorax broad and narrowing to front. 3–4mm.
SHOOT & STEM	Egg gallery straight, longitudinal with irregular brood chamber at base. Maturation feeding of beetle in current year's shoots causing 'spire tops' through repeated shoot pruning and also flattened crowns. Breeding in weakened trees and fresh-felled produce. Entry into green trees often marked by 'resin tubes'. Overwintering often in short galleries at ground level below litter layer.	Black to pitchy-red beetle. Head and thorax shining black. 3–5mm.
SHOOT & STEM	Egg gallery two-armed with central brood chamber, transverse. Larval tunnels very short. Maturation as for above species. Confined to Scotland and the New Forest.	Dark brown to pitchy. Head and thorax black. 3.5–4mm.

TIME OF DAMAGE	STAGE	ORDER AND FAMILY	LATIN NAME	ENGLISH NAME	TYPE OF CROP	DAMAGE RATING (see key p.12)	REFER-ENCE
Spring/early summer	MITE	ACARI Eriophyidae	*Trisetacus pini*	Pine twig gall mite	Pole	X	116
All year round	NYMPH & ADULT	HEMIPTERA Adelgidae	*Pineus strobi*	Weymouth pine woolly aphid	Pole & older	XX	50
April to Sept.	ADULT & LARVA	COLEOPTERA Curculionidae	*Pissodes castaneus*	Small banded pine weevil	Pole & younger	XXXX	3 65
April to Sept.	ADULT & LARVA	COLEOPTERA Curculionidae	*Pissodes pini*	Banded pine weevil	All ages	XX	29
All year round Adult peak March/May & Aug./Sept.	ADULT & LARVA	COLEOPTERA Scolytidae	*Hylastes ater* Plates 38 and 79 See also pp.135–6	Black pine beetle	Trans-plants	XXXX	121 104
May to Sept.	LARVA	COLEOPTERA Scolytidae	*Hylurgops palliatus* Plate 81		Felled produce	X	117
May to Sept.	ADULT & LARVA	COLEOPTERA Scolytidae	*Tomicus piniperda* Plates 72 and 94 See also p.124	Pine shoot beetle	All ages	XXX	15 72
March/April to June/July	ADULT & LARVA	COLEOPTERA Scolytidae	*Tomicus minor*	Lesser pine shoot beetle	All ages	X	15

PART OF TREE	DESCRIPTION OF DAMAGE AND FEEDING HABIT	DESCRIPTION OF DAMAGING STAGE *(see note on p.12)*
STEM	Egg gallery star-shaped and up to 10-or-more-armed. Larval tunnels on alternate sides and very short. Blue-staining fungi are carried by the mother beetle. Said to be secondary except when allowed to breed up in fellings or windblown stems and then can be aggressive.	Adult dark brown to reddish brown. Excavation at rear irregular, shining and with sides toothed. 2–3.5mm.
YOUNG STEM OR TWIG	Egg gallery diminutive, star-shaped and 3-or-more-armed. Attacks green twigs up to 1cm diameter, often ring-barking and killing them.	Tiny dark red-brown beetle. 1–1.8mm.
STEM	Egg gallery star-shaped and 3–5-armed with central brood chamber. Maturation within gallery. Common small beetle attacking dead young trees and small felling waste.	Dark brown to black with reddish brown wing covers. 1.5–2.5mm. Distinct excavation at hind end.
STEM	Gallery system within the bark. Egg gallery star-shaped with central brood chamber and a number of arms to the star.	Red brown with dark head. 1.5–3mm. Distinct toothed excavation at hind end.
STEM	Egg gallery immensely long (up to 1 metre), usually 2, 3 or 4-armed with central brood chamber. Maturation feeding an extension of the pupal chamber. Breeds in felled timber and recorded on weakened trees. A southern and introduced species.	Light to dark brown. 5.5–8mm. Very pronounced toothed and hairy excavation at hind end.
STEM	Gallery system short and very irregular, often many-armed with chambered larval galleries.	Brown to black. 3.5–5mm. Distinct toothed excavation at hind end.
STEM	Egg gallery longitudinal and very long (up to 75cm), sometimes sinuous, with hooked brood chamber at base. Normally attacks weakly and dying trees but becomes aggressive on green trees when allowed to breed up. Associated with a wilt fungus (*Ceratocystis montia*). Pitch or resin tubes on the stem are diagnostic.	Stout black cylindrical beetle. 4–7.5mm.
STEM	Egg gallery a long chamber and larvae feed communally. Entry holes are marked with red pitch-tubes. Seldom kills trees but can become aggressive at high densities.	Very large reddish brown beetle. 5–9mm.

TIME OF DAMAGE	STAGE	ORDER AND FAMILY	LATIN NAME	ENGLISH NAME	TYPE OF CROP	DAMAGE RATING *(see key p.12)*	REFER-ENCE
May to Aug. or spring	ADULT & LARVA	COLEOPTERA Scolytidae	*Ips acuminatus* Plate 82		Young thicket	XXX	14 15
May to July	LARVA	COLEOPTERA Scolytidae	*Pityophthorus pubescens*	Pine twig bark beetle	Pole & older	X	
May to July	LARVA	COLEOPTERA Scolytidae	*Pityogenes bidentatus* Plate 87	Two-toothed pine beetle	All ages of thin barked produce	X	117
Spring/ summer	LARVA	COLEOPTERA Scolytidae	*Pityogenes chalcographus* Plate 88	Pine bark beetle	Thin barked felled produce	X	117
April/May to Aug.	LARVA	COLEOPTERA Scolytidae	*Ips sexdentatus*	Six-toothed bark beetle	Large produce	XX	15 61
May to June & Aug. to May	LARVA	COLEOPTERA Scolytidae	*Orthotomicus laricis* Plate 86	Pattern engraver beetle	Pole to large produce	X	117
June/July/Aug.	LARVA	COLEOPTERA Scolytidae	*Dendroctonus ponderosae**	Mountain pine beetle	All ages	XXXXX*	147 155
Spring/ summer	LARVA	COLEOPTERA Scolytidae	*Dendroctonus valens**	Red turpentine beetle	All ages	XXXX*	147 155

PART OF TREE	DESCRIPTION OF DAMAGE AND FEEDING HABIT	DESCRIPTION OF DAMAGING STAGE *(see note on p.12)*
ROOT	Yellowing and death of patches of plants in seedbeds and transplant lines. Very common on container plants when under-watering may be suspected as predisposing factor. Aphids on roots amongst bluish waxy wool.	White aphid in wool.
WOOD	In felled logs and stumps, usually in rotting wood. Often after *Asemum* or *Arhopalus* have left. Tunnel deep into the wood. Cycle 2 years.	Larva a longhorn. 34mm. Adult with two oblique yellow stripes on wing covers. 12–22mm.

PSEUDOTSUGA (DOUGLAS FIR)

NEEDLE	Successive spring and summer generations feeding on undersides of needles causes localised yellowing and characteristic bending and twisting. Can severely reduce growth in young stock.	Small blackish grey aphid with waxy wool and honeydew.
SEED	Eats out the contents of seed. On emergence leaves small round hole in seed. Can account for a high proportion of seed particularly in an otherwise poor seed year.	Larva a small gall wasp. 2mm. Adult yellow.
WOOD	Larva bores wandering tunnels of increasing diameter into wood mainly in a radial direction. Tunnels are discoloured with fungus introduced by the female. Ejects huge quantities of frass.	Cream larva with a swordlike process at tail. Hump behind head. 6–18mm. Adult long, slender yellow-brown to dark brown. 6–18mm.

TAXUS (YEW)

NEEDLE	'Artichoke' gall, green with nearly white centre at first, later turning brown. Terminal and persistent.	Orange-red larva. 2–3mm.

TIME OF DAMAGE	STAGE	ORDER AND FAMILY	LATIN NAME	ENGLISH NAME	TYPE OF CROP	DAMAGE RATING *(see key p.12)*	REFER-ENCE
All year round	NYMPH & ADULT	HEMIPTERA Pemphigidae	*Stagona pini*	Pine root aphid	All nursery stock	XXX	116
Adults May to July	LARVA	COLEOPTERA Cerambycidae	*Rhagium bifasciatum*		Old wood	X	75

TIME OF DAMAGE	STAGE	ORDER AND FAMILY	LATIN NAME	ENGLISH NAME	TYPE OF CROP	DAMAGE RATING	REFER-ENCE
Spring & early summer	ADULT & LARVA	HEMIPTERA Adelgidae	*Adelges cooleyi* Plate 3	Douglas fir woolly aphid	All ages	XXXX	50
July to May	LARVA	HYMENOPTERA Torymidae	*Megastigmus spermotrophus* Plate 45	Douglas fir seed wasp	Seed bearers	XXXXX	128 129
June/July	LARVA	COLEOPTERA Lymexylidae	*Hylecoetus dermestoides* Plate 40	Large timberworm	Logs & stumps	XXX	39 40

TIME OF DAMAGE	STAGE	ORDER AND FAMILY	LATIN NAME	ENGLISH NAME	TYPE OF CROP	DAMAGE RATING	REFER-ENCE
May/June	LARVA	DIPTERA Cecidomyiidae	*Taxomyia taxi*	Yew gall midge	All ages	XX	114

Plate 1
Aceria erineus.
Gall on walnut leaves.

Plate 2
Adelges abietis.
Gall on Norway spruce.

Plate 3
Adelges cooleyi.
Gall on Sitka spruce.

Plate 4
Adelges laricis.
Gall on Sitka spruce.

Plate 5
Adelges nordmannianae.
Leaf curl on Cilician fir.

Plate 6
Agrotis segetum.
Ring-barking of sycamore seedlings.

Plate 7
Andricus fecundator.
Artichoke gall on oak bud.

Plate 8
Andricus quercuscalicis.
Gall on oak.

Plate 9
Anoplonyx destructor.
Larva on larch.

Plate 10
Apocheima pilosaria.
Larva on oak.

11

12

Plate 11
Arhopalus tristis.
Larvae in wood.

Plate 12
Artacris macrorhynchus.
Galls on *Acer.*

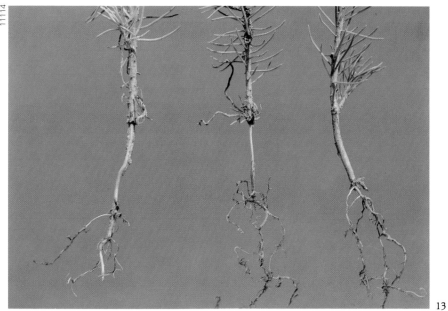

13

Plate 13
Barypeithes pellucidus.
Ring-barking of seedlings.

Plate 14
Bourletiella hortensis.
Distortion of cotyledons of Lodgepole pine

Plate 15
Brachonyx pineti.
Adult and feeding damage on Lodgepole pine needles.

Plate 16
Bupalus piniaria.
Larva on Scots pine.

Plate 17
Caliroa annulipes.
Surface feeding damage on oak leaves.

Plate 18
Cephalcia lariciphila.
Larva feeding on larch needles.

Plate 19
Chrysomela populi.
Larva on poplar.

Plate 20
Coleophora laricella.
Mined larch needles.

Plate 21
Contarinia baeri.
Needle damage on Scots pine.

94

Plate 22
Croesus septentrionalis.
Larvae.

Plate 23
Cryptococcus fagisuga.
Wool-covered colonies on beech.

Plate 24
Cryptorhynchus lapathi.
Larva in wood of willow.

Plate 25
Curculio nucum.
Larva emerged from hollowed acorn.

37201

26

3211

27

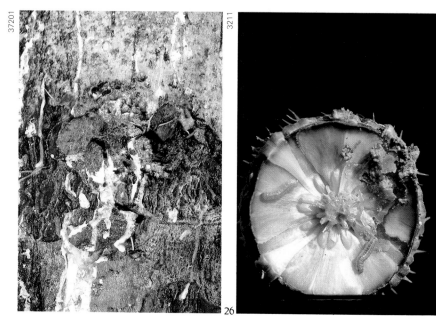

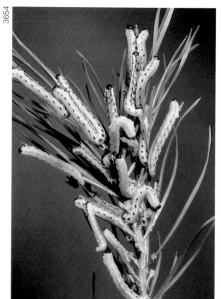

Plate 26
Dendroctonus micans.
Fresh resin tubes on Sitka spruce.

Plate 27
Dioryctria abietella.
Larvae in damaged *Abies* cone.

3654

28

Plate 28
Diprion pini.
Larvae on Scots pine.

Plate 29
Dolichorhynchus microphasmis.
Death of Sitka spruce seedlings.

29

Plate 30
Dysaphis aucupariae.
Damage on leaves of Wild service tree.

Plate 31
Elatobium abietinum.
Characteristic defoliation of Sitka spruce.

30

31

Plate 32
Epinotia tedella.
Needles of Norway spruce mined and spun together.

Plate 33
Erannis defoliaria.
Larva on oak leaf.

Plate 34
Euproctis chrysorrhoea.
Larva on hawthorn leaves.

32

33

34

35

36

Plate 35
Gilpinia hercyniae.
Larva on Sitka spruce needles.

Plate 36
Gypsonoma aceriana.
Frass ejected at axil of poplar leaf.

37

38

Plate 37
Hepialus humuli.
Spiral tunnel on oak transplant root.

Plate 38
Hylastes ater.
Ring-barking of Scots pine transplants.

Plate 40
Hylecoetus dermestoides.
Larval tunnels in Douglas fir wood.

40

39

41

Plate 39
Hylobius abietis.
Adult weevils on Scots pine shoot.

Plate 41
Ips cembrae.
Attack on green larch trees.

42

43

Plate 42
Ips typographus.
Attack on green Norway spruce trees.

Plate 43
Leperisinus varius.
The gallery system.

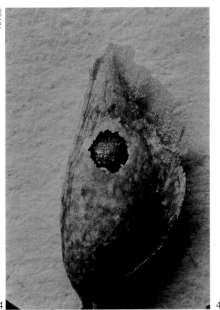

44

45

Plate 44
Leucoma salicis.
Larvae on poplar.

Plate 45
Megastigmus spermotrophus.
Larva in Douglas fir seed.

20362

2474

46

47

Plate 46
Moritziella corticalis.
Feeding effects on oak cambium.

Plate 47
Neodiprion sertifer.
Larvae on Scots pine.

34226

48

Plate 48
Neuroterus numismalis.
Galls on oak leaves.

Plate 49
Neuroterus quercusbaccarum.
Galls on male flowers of oak.

49

50

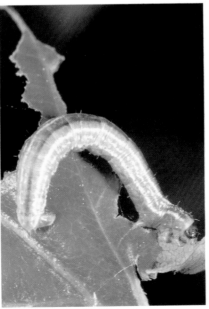

51

Plate 50
Oligonychus ununguis.
Eggs on young Norway spruce shoots.

Plate 51
Operophtera brumata.
Larva on oak.

Plate 52
Otiorhynchus singularis.
Ring-barking of shoots.

Plate 54
Pachypappa tremulae.
Aphids on Norway spruce roots.

Plate 53
Pachynematus imperfectus.
Larva on larch.

37196

55

Plate 55
Panolis flammea.
Larvae on Lodgepole pine.

35908

56

Plate 56
Pemphigus bursarius.
Galls on poplar petioles.

Plate 57
Phalera bucephala.
Larvae on beech.

Plate 59
Phyllodecta vitellinae.
Larvae on poplar.

57

59

Plate 58
Phyllaphis fagi.
Wool-covered colonies on beech leaf.

58

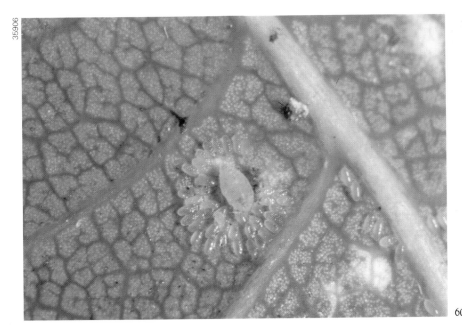

60

Plate 60
Phylloxera glabra.
Aphid and eggs on underside of oak leaf.

61

62

Plate 61
Pissodes strobi.
Shoot death and crown distortion of
Sitka spruce.

Plate 62
Pristiphora abietina.
Larvae on Norway spruce.

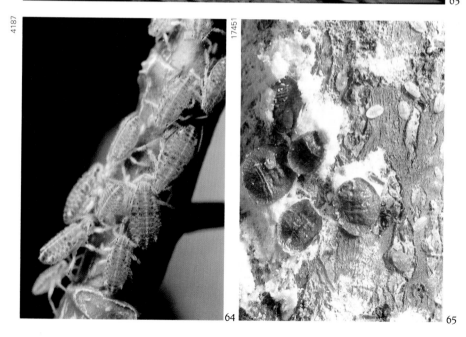

1474

Plate 63
Pristiphora wesmaeli.
Larva on larch.

4187

17451

Plate 64
Pterocomma sp.
Aphids on willow stem.

Plate 65
Pulvinaria regalis.
Horse chestnut scale.

63

64

65

66

67

68

69

Plate 66
Rhyacionia buoliana.
'Resin tent' near Scots pine bud.

Plate 67
Rhynchaenus fagi.
Larval mine and adult shot holes on beech.

Plate 68
Scolytus scolytus.
Maturation feeding in elm branch crotch.

Plate 69
Strophosomus melanogrammus.
Ring-barking of shoots.

Plate 70
Tetraneura ulmi.
Gall on elm.

70

Plate 71
Tetropium gabrieli.
Larva in larch wood.

71

37195

72

Plate 72
Tomicus piniperda.
Resin tubes in Lodgepole pine.

3213

73

Plate 73
Xyloterus lineatus.
Gallery in Japanese larch wood.

74

Plate 74
Zeiraphera diniana.
Damage to current shoots of
Lodgepole pine.

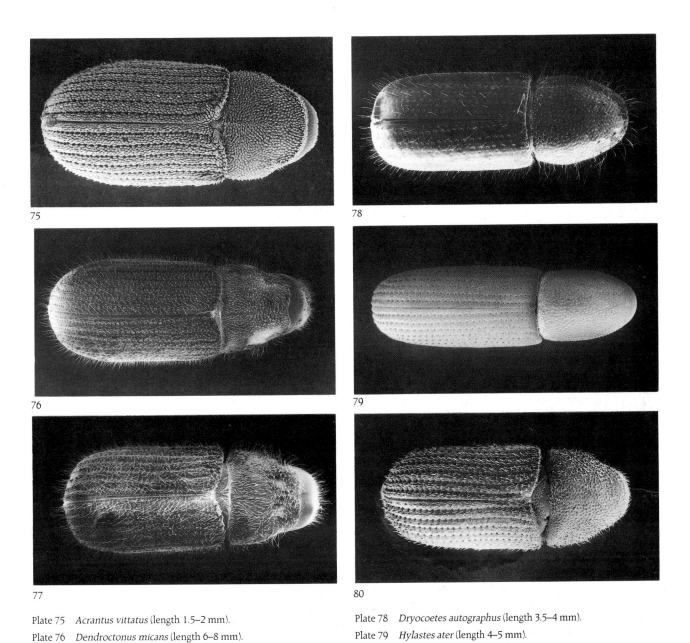

Plate 75   *Acrantus vittatus* (length 1.5–2 mm).

Plate 76   *Dendroctonus micans* (length 6–8 mm).

Plate 77   *Dendroctonus rufipennis* (length 4–7 mm).

Plate 78   *Dryocoetes autographus* (length 3.5–4 mm).

Plate 79   *Hylastes ater* (length 4–5 mm).

Plate 80   *Hylurgopinus rufipes* (length 2.5–3 mm).

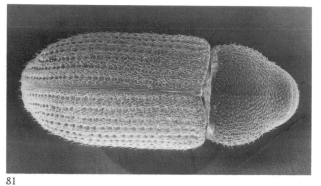

81

84

82

85

83

86

Plate 81   *Hylurgops palliatus* (length 3–4 mm).

Plate 82   *Ips acuminatus* (length 2–3.5 mm).

Plate 83   *Ips cembrae* (length 5–6 mm).

Plate 84   *Ips typographus* (length 4.5–5 mm).

Plate 85   *Leperisinus varius* (length 2.5–3 mm).

Plate 86   *Orthotomicus laricis* (length 3.5–5 mm).

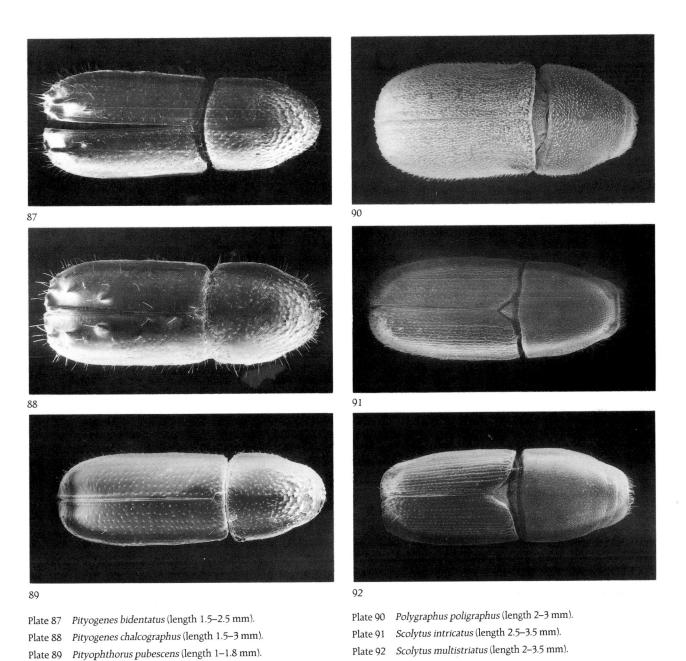

87

88

89

90

91

92

Plate 87   *Pityogenes bidentatus* (length 1.5–2.5 mm).

Plate 88   *Pityogenes chalcographus* (length 1.5–3 mm).

Plate 89   *Pityophthorus pubescens* (length 1–1.8 mm).

Plate 90   *Polygraphus poligraphus* (length 2–3 mm).

Plate 91   *Scolytus intricatus* (length 2.5–3.5 mm).

Plate 92   *Scolytus multistriatus* (length 2–3.5 mm).

93

94

95

96

97

98

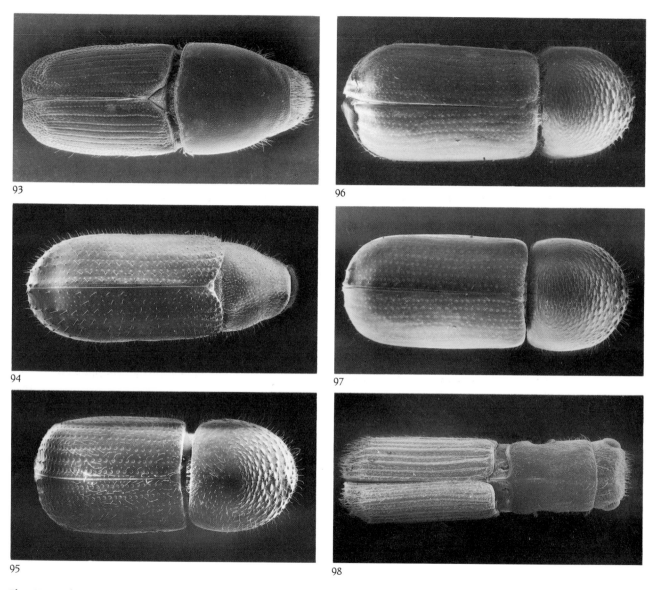

Plate 93 *Scolytus scolytus* (length 3–6 mm).
Plate 94 *Tomicus piniperda* (length 3–5 mm).
Plate 95 *Xyleborus dispar* (length 3–3.5 mm).

Plate 96 *Xyloterus domesticus* (length 3–4 mm).
Plate 97 *Xyloterus lineatus* (length 3–3.5 mm).
Plate 98 *Platypus cylindrus* (length 5–5.5 mm).

Part Two: Principal Forest Pests

Scolytidae

Bark beetles are essentially insects of woody host plants and are perhaps the one group which can fairly be regarded as truly forest insects. Whilst a few are specific to certain shrubs or climbers such as *Hedera* (Ivy), *Sarothamnus* (Broom) or *Clematis*, most attack tree species. They tend all more or less equally to come under suspicion for their supposed ability to take advantage of the forester when he is in the greatest of difficulties – after a fire, windblow, drought or defoliating insect. Such a wholesale blackening of the whole family is not justified but a feature they do have in common is that all are secondary to some other debilitating primary factor. They differ greatly, however, in their degree of aggressiveness, their habits and in their choice of well-defined environmental niche. Each has a life style of its own and it is this that determines a species' importance to forestry and ecological significance. These differences must be understood if each is to be placed in perspective.

The subject may conveniently be discussed within the context of a generalised bark beetle life cycle. The first adult beetles to attack a tree are normally referred to as the 'pioneers'. There is divergence of opinion as to the mechanism involved in bringing these pioneers to a susceptible tree. It may be that the endemic population of the species, in the breeding phase, continually searches at random in some way testing for host plants in a receptive condition. It could also be that ailing, susceptible hosts emit chemical signals, the so-called 'primary attractant', which guide the seeking adult directly to the target. Perhaps both mechanisms are at work within the family. The pioneer beetles may either be males or females depending on the species involved but it will always be a particular sex for a given species.

The boring of the pioneer and the passage of host plant material through its gut produce 'the secondary attractant', a set of chemicals, the aggregation pheromone, which constitutes a 'come hither' signal to both sexes of the same species[41, 102]. The pheromone is typically a mixture of chemicals, some of them unchanged host plant products such as terpenes and some modified by processes within the beetle. There is an immediate exception, however, to this generalization in the case of

Dendroctonus micans in which it appears that there is no aggregation pheromone, at least not one operating in the adult stage.

With the arrival of the pioneer and the meeting up of the sexes comes initiation of the gallery system. This will typically start with a widened, often characteristically shaped, brood chamber where mating takes place. From the chamber extend one or more egg (or mother) galleries. The female lays her eggs singly or in groups on both sides of each gallery, in niches. In monogamous species, such as *Tomicus piniperda* or *Hylastes* spp., there is a single egg gallery; polygamous species such as *Ips* have one per female reaching an extreme case in *Ips acuminatus* which, under certain circumstances, may have upwards of 12–15 egg galleries[14].

When eggs hatch each larva extends the system outwards from the egg gallery. There are many variations on this theme and each is characteristic of a particular species; larval galleries differ in shape, length and direction and also in their placement in stem tissue, i.e. mostly in the wood, partly in the wood and partly in the cambium/phloem region, or totally in the bark. Each larval tunnel increases in width as the larva grows until it terminates in a pupal chamber. Here the insect develops finally into an adult.

The point of emergence is another variable feature. Adults, on reaching maturity, may escape by boring through the bark roof of the pupal chamber giving the typical 'shot-hole' effect, others may use a common place of emergence and others may leave at any convenient spot offered through collapse of the gallery roof. *D. micans* again shows strong deviation from the norm. An already fertilised female makes the attack. She bores out a long, broad brood chamber which she packs with bore meal (or frass) into which she lays batches of eggs. The larvae eat out a large patch, feeding 'line abreast', compacting the frass behind them in a characteristically quilt-like pattern. They pupate in the quilt and all emerge through a few holes bored in the roof above them. Since the female pioneer emits no aggregation pheromone her gallery system may be solitary, whereas in most other species a single successful attack is followed by many others.

Important variations between species exist in the so-called maturation feeding phase of newly emerged adults which takes place before they commence breeding. It may occur as an extension of the larval gallery system, the beetles leaving the pupal chamber to make further borings to feed before flight. In other species it takes place after emergence and flight and often in some part of the green tree so that, in this phase, there is no reason to suggest that the attack is other than primary. Many species of forest importance are in this latter category, e.g. *Scolytus* spp. (Plate 68), *Tomicus* spp., *Ips cembrae* and *Hylastes* spp. The feeding in the first three species is in the crown of healthy trees and in the last typically at the root collar of transplants or regeneration but also may be in roots of larger trees or underside of thin-bark fresh-felled logs. In some, as in the last three, the behaviour seems to be obligatory but in others, such as the *Scolytus* spp., merely facultative in that the beetles appear sometimes to feed in shoots and sometimes during the initial stages of boring out the egg gallery (leaving the first few centimetres without egg niches).

There is also a rather special and again facultative type of feeding sometimes referred to as 'bad weather feeding' in which huge numbers of beetles of both sexes collect in dense patches all in their own short gallery. This behaviour may occasionally be seen in some *Hylastes* spp. and is a common feature, for instance, in *Ips typographus* of mainland Europe. Its part in beetle survival has not been fully explained but the behaviour does seem to occur when beetles have emerged, are all ready for flight and breeding, but are suddenly overtaken by adverse weather conditions. These aggregations of beetles do seem superficially at least to have something in common with the smaller over-wintering aggregations of *T. piniperda* found in short irregular tunnels at the base of pine, or the 'bark roses' of *Leperisinus fraxini* in *Fraxinus* or *Acrantus (Ptelobius) vittatus* in *Ulmus*.

There are two further characteristics of bark beetles which are often closely associated and are most important to appreciate. The first is the inherent aggressiveness of a given species and the second the nature of any fungal associations it may have[66, 149]. Certainly some species are more aggressive in the breeding phase than others and will attack a debilitated but still green tree, e.g. *I. cembrae* (Plate 41) or *T. piniperda*. Some, on the other hand, will only attack dead or felled trees, e.g. *Hylurgops*

palliatus, *Dryocoetus autographus* or *Dryocoetinus villosus*, etc. The extreme is found in some of the wood-inhabiting 'ambrosia' species which will enter the tree only some time after death, e.g. *Xyloterus (Trypodendron)* spp. Certain associated fungi, however, can apparently change the relative aggressiveness of a beetle species (although it would perhaps be more reasonable to treat such cases as specialised interaction phenomena).

Associations between fungi and bark beetles may take many different forms, from the simple, apparently inadvertent, carriage of spores as in the elm Scolytids (rather as a pollinating insect may transfer pollen from one flower to another) to the highly specialised relationship of the ambrosia beetle. In the latter case specific fungi are carried in special structures (mycangia) on the mother beetle for culture in the tunnel system as food for her larval brood.

There are also a variety of very complex and poorly understood relationships between certain bark beetle species and specific wilt fungi including 'bluestains' and yeasts. *Tomicus minor* and *Ips acuminatus*, for instance, seem to have gone some way down the ambrosial trail in that they have retained their phloem-feeding, true bark beetle status, but feed their larvae almost, if not entirely, on fungus cultured in shortish, stubby larval galleries. The fungus involved, is said to be a species of *Ophiostoma*[103], a group of fungi well known to be aggressive and to cause wilt. *Trichosporium tingens* has also been reported as closely associated with *I. acuminatus* in Scotland[113]. Certainly the two beetles, although normally of secondary importance only, at normal population levels, are capable of attack on green trees when allowed to breed up to high density in windblown or felled timber. The change in the beetles' behaviour takes place at the same time as the greatly increased invasion of the cambial area by bluestain. However, the relationship between insect and fungi is not well understood. Nor has it been adequately demonstrated that it is a single fungus species that both feeds the larva and attacks trees.

A very much more potent association of a similar kind exists in some N. American species of *Dendroctonus* and perhaps also in *Ips cembrae*[112] and *I. typographus*[63]. Here again we have common species typically found attacking dead and dying trees at low endemic levels of population. Any attempt to invade a healthy tree at such levels will result in individuals being 'pitched out' or drowned in resin and wounds will be cut off internally by the tree with a fungistatic barrier of resin and wound tissue[63, 111]. Stress factors, whether from drought, damage or crop competition, reduce the tree's ability directly to withstand beetle attack in this way. Wound reaction is a high energy-demanding process and can become inadequate if beetle numbers and attacks increase over some critical point[64]. Specific, very aggressive, wilt fungi are carried by these beetle species and in some cases in identifiable mycangia. Having defeated the tree's internal wound reaction mechanism the wilt fungus proceeds to kill the tree very quickly indeed. In this way, of course, fresh substrate is made available to the species for breeding purposes and a chain reaction ensues.

A bark beetle may thus be a pest because it is:

(a) an intrinsically aggressive species (i.e. will attack green trees under stress through drought, defoliation or damage),
e.g. *Ips cembrae* (Plate 41), *Tomicus piniperda*, *Dendroctonus micans* and *Ips typographus** (Plate 42);

(b) an intrinsically non-aggressive species attacking dead, dying and felled trees but having a type of maturation feeding directly causing death or deformity of trees,
e.g. *Hylastes* spp. (Plate 38) and *T. piniperda*;

(c) an intrinsically non-aggressive species attacking dead, dying and felled trees, but having fungal associates which can overcome the trees defences at high beetle density,
e.g. some N. American species of *Dendroctonus*;
or
carries a fungus essential for the nutrition of its larvae and which may at high density, become itself aggressive,
e.g. *Ips acuminatus* and *Tomicus minor*;

(d) an intrinsically non-aggressive species attacking dead, dying and felled trees, but having a type of maturation feeding phase harmless in itself but during which it may vector an aggressive fungus,
e.g. elm *Scolytus* spp.
N.B. *S. intricatus* is also a potential vector of a disease such as Oak wilt[89], having a convenient maturation feeding behaviour. Both *Leperesinus fraxini* on ash and *Acrantus vittatus* on *Ulmus* feed in 'bark roses' and must be potential vectors (the latter species has been claimed as a vector of Dutch elm disease in other countries but not so far in Britain);

(e) an ambrosia beetle, together with its associated fungus, causing technical degrade of timber, e.g. *Xyloterus lineatus* (Plate 73) or the closely allied platypodid, *Platypus cylindrus*[10].

Scolytus scolytus, S. multistriatus, S. laevis

History

Neither of the two native species, *Scolytus scolytus* and *S. multistriatus* nor the recently recorded *S. laevis*[8] can claim pest status on their own account. They are all, however, vectors of Dutch elm disease.

Life cycles

S. scolytus, the Large elm bark beetle. One and a half, exceptionally two, generations a year[88].

Adults – April/May and July/August into September
Eggs   – April/May and July/September
Larvae – May/June and August through winter to spring
Pupae – June/July and August/September

S. multistriatus, the Small elm bark beetle. One generation a year[88].

Adults – June and over-wintering
Eggs   – June
Larvae – July through winter
Pupae – May/June

S. laevis

Said to be similar to *S. scolytus* in Scandinavia.

Forest importance

This group of bark beetles will invade only dying trees or felled material in their breeding phase. After emergence adult beetles enter a period of maturation feeding either on healthy twigs in the crown or immediately on re-entry into logs or stems of dying trees for breeding purposes. In either case they may carry spores of *Ceratocystis ulmi*, the Dutch elm disease fungus. In the twig type of maturation feeding the fungus carried to the healthy crown may enter the vascular system and cause disease to travel downwards and outwards through the tree, predisposing it to later occupation by beetles for breeding. Thus there is a cyclic pattern of attack and potentially a logarithmic increase in populations of both organisms, beetle and fungus. In the stem-to-stem pattern of attack one can only assume that either invasion can only take place on the already predisposed tree or, that repeated attempted attacks upon a green tree can successfully breach the tree's defences against both beetle and fungus.

Dendroctonus micans

History

D. micans is the only European representative of this essentially N. American genus. It was first recorded in Britain in 1982 and indications then were that it had been in the country unnoticed since at least 1973[32]. The beetle has established itself in most parts of Wales and western margins of the neighbouring counties of England with one outlier some 100 km north.

Life cycle

Variable as to development time but mostly 12–18 months. All stages may be found at most times of the year. The cycle appears to be strongly influenced by seasonal climatic conditions.

Adult   – All year round
Eggs   – May to November
Larvae   – All year round
Pupae   – Spring–autumn

Forest importance

The bark beetle is unique in behavioural characteristics amongst European species. It normally attacks only the green, albeit stressed, tree and must, therefore, be regarded as a very aggressive species. However, since the pioneering beetle is an already fertilised female and emits no aggregation pheromone its successful entry into a tree evokes no mass attack as it would in most other bark beetle species. Despite being aggressive, the species is not an efficient or quick tree-killer except when stress is harsh and populations become high. The sum of independently made single attacks and resulting cumulative damage to the cambium may become critical to the tree's survival. At endemic level the large chamber-like brood system (see under Scolytidae – Bark beetles, p.118) is occluded with wound tissue subsequent to emergence of the brood and, after some years, may be discernible only by a slight flattening of the stem, or canker-like area of roughened bark with or without some resin flow.

Picea abies in Britain has so far proved more immediately attractive to the beetle but the tree has demonstrated an ability to survive many years' successive attacks. Whilst appearing intrinsically less attractive, *S. sitchensis* seems to succumb after only 3 or 4 years' attack. In Denmark and Holland outbreaks in the 1940s and 50s seem to have been very much more dramatic and entire crops of *P. sitchensis* are reported to have been lost[25, 92]. Damage to *P. abies* in the latter part of the last century in Belgium is also well documented and it does seem that whilst there are certain features of outbreak common to all, no very precise pattern appears. Certainly drought on dryer sites receives repeated mention in the literature as a precursor to invasion.

Rhizophagus grandis, a predator beetle, specific to *D. micans* has also been regularly reported to have a fine appetite for both eggs and larvae. However, as is so often the case in natural enemies suspected to be important in limiting population increase at low levels, there is a lack of means to back suspicion of efficacy with quantitative proof. In this context the species' ubiquity in *D. micans* broods throughout the predator's distribution in mainland Europe must be counted in its favour whilst its failure to control numbers at outbreak level is to be expected with a low density specialist and particularly with a late arrival.

D. micans has commonly announced its slow advance across mainland Europe by an initial explosive first appearance in new territory. It has then settled to quieter and relatively unobtrusive colonisation[25]. This could be taken as circumstantial evidence for the appearance of some unspecified natural control, such as *R. grandis*, following on the heels of the enemy. It could be the case, of course, that *D. micans* first decimates those crops most susceptible to it and is then reduced to less favourable niches – at this stage its natural enemies could be reduced from the critically important to a less obviously significant status.

LARGE LARCH BARK BEETLE Plates 41 & 83 (see also p.67).

Ips cembrae

History

The beetle was first recorded in Britain in 1955[68, 133] in the Scottish counties of Moray, Nairn, Banff and Inverness. Since then it has reached south as far as Peebles and has shown up more or less wherever larch is present in the north. The larches are exotics of long standing and, together with the native Scots Pine, have been used widely in plantations since the 18th century. It is instructive to note in a plant health context therefore, that this widely distributed and aggressive European beetle, so evidently adapted to Scottish conditions, took such a very long time to establish a toe-hold.

Life cycle[133]

Adult	–	There are normally two broods in the year and perhaps a partial second generation, April/May and July/August
Eggs	–	May/June and August/September
Larvae	–	May/July and September through winter
Pupae	–	June/July

Maturation feeding in 2 to 6-year-old branches after adult emergence.

Forest importance

We have yet to learn the final distribution of this beetle in Britain. It is reputed to be a secondary species in native European larch plantations breeding in felled logs, windblown stems and dying trees. Droughty conditions on dryer sites are said to promote attack on green trees. Such a model appears to find some confirmation in Scottish experience in that the apparently more aggressive attacks on older trees and, in one or two cases, upon younger newly thinned crops have mostly occurred in lower rainfall areas north and east of the Grampians. A less hostile role, however, has proved more the rule in central Perthshire and wetter parts. The species has been found to breed successfully in a number of conifers including windblown *P. sitchensis* still on its roots. Shoots of *Pseudotsuga* as well as those of *Larix* spp. may also be attacked in the maturation feeding phase. The beetle's reaction to trees defoliated by the sawflies *Cephalcia lariciphila* or *Anoplonyx destructor* has not been put to the test.

Tomicus piniperda

History

Pine shoot beetle (together with the pine and spruce infesting species *Hylurgops palliatus*) must be among the commonest scolytids in Britain. Its early reputation as a pest to be feared in all pine plantations has not been entirely justified although its aggressive attack on droughted or defoliated trees can be a serious cause of widespread mortality.

Life cycle[72]

Adults	–	Present most of the year; overwinters in short tunnels at base of trees or in shoots
Eggs	–	February/March to May or early June
Larvae	–	May to early July
Pupae	–	June to early July

Forest importance

T. piniperda breeds in most categories of freshly dead, dying and felled produce. It appears generally to maintain a high level of endemic population and is thus always poised to take advantage of calamity. Trees completely defoliated by the Pine looper *Bupalus piniaria* are attacked and killed as a matter of course. Trees subject to stress, for instance those growing on sand dunes, may also be attacked whilst still in a green and apparently healthy condition. Similarly prone are young crops subject to premature brashing or other forms of green pruning. Felled larch may also be attacked successfully. On the other hand even severe shoot pruning by the self-same beetle species in its maturation feeding phase appears not to predispose the trees to attack for breeding. Pine suffering quick death and fast deterioration through the root fungus *Heterobasidion (Fomes) annosus*[91], so typical of some crops in East Anglia, seem to support the weevil *Pissodes castaneus* rather than *T. piniperda*. *P. contorta* completely defoliated by Pine beauty moth *Panolis flammea* remain unattacked and perhaps timing of damage and speed of drying out are critical factors in these cases.

T. piniperda is not quite so catholic in its acceptance of breeding substrate as at first it seems. Experiments have shown that fellings made in late August into September remain relatively immune from attack, being too late for the current year's crop of beetles and too dry for the next season's brood. This window is short and not very useful in normal forest practice but has provided a strategy for limiting increase in small fellings where interference with the environment needs to be kept to the minimum.

CONIFER AMBROSIA BEETLE Plates 73 & 97 (see also p.61).

Xyloterus (Trypodendron) lineatus

History

The blackened tunnels which mark this beetle's journey into the wood of a wide range of conifers have long been familiar to growers and sawmillers alike, particularly to those in the wetter parts of the country. The beetles are essentially inhabitors of timber rather than the growing tree and are regarded therefore as 'technical pests' responsible for localised degrade of produce.

Life cycle[27]

Adult	–	Attacks late April to end of June; overwinters in the soil
Eggs	–	May/June
Larvae	–	May/July
Pupae	–	June/July/beginning of August

Forest importance

A forest in full and sustained production is likely from time to time to experience accumulations of felled produce either through difficulties of extraction brought on by adverse weather conditions or some form of market failure. Emergency salvage fellings following windblow or other unpredictable occurrences can similarly bring about deviations from normal procedures. The beetle maintains an endemic population in felled stem waste, windbroken 'spikes' and to some degree in larger stumps; this population will therefore be small in the young or unworked forest.

The species has an outstandingly powerful pheromone which aggregates individuals very efficiently. This is a useful characteristic in that, at normal low population levels, attacking adults tend to be concentrated on one or two logs only. At higher levels, however, attack becomes more general and the philosophy of control will then depend much on the market for which the timber is intended. Normally the pulp market will have few objections to infested material. Poles are similarly little affected particularly if they are to be treated with preservatives. Saw mills may take a very different view, on the other hand.

The beetle has a known predilection for logs felled during the winter months December to February prior to adult appearance, those felled earlier or later showing a much lower degree of susceptibility. Removal of logs in the susceptible class before beetle attack commences in April provides an effective silvicultural control strategy, whilst normal felling operations can continue during flight of the beetle without fear of attack. Chemical control prior to attack is effective and provides a back-up when it proves impossible to circumvent trouble by careful timing of operations.

Bupalus piniaria

An indigenous species on *Pinus sylvestris* and, like *Panolis flammea*, a widespread and serious pest on heathlands in mainland Europe. Localised complete defoliation was experienced in Britain in plantation forest for the first time at Cannock in 1953. Subsequently outbreaks have occurred in the Midlands, in the north-east of England and in central and eastern Scotland, with control operations in the years 1954, 1957, 1963, 1970, 1977, 1979 and 1984.

Life cycle[31]

Adult	– End of May to end of June
Eggs	– In rows on the needles in June/July
Larvae	– Early June to Oct./Nov. on old needles
Pupae	– Beneath the litter layer, normally between mineral and organic layers some 2cm deep from autumn to May/June.

Forest importance

The species, although destructive when it strikes in Britain, is plainly approaching the margin of its distribution as a pest. Some indication of its relative success in our environment may be had from the average weight of female pupae which are some ½–⅔rds that of their counterpart in central Germany; its fecundity is, therefore, lower and thus is its potential speed of increase. Outbreaks tend to be local rather than regional, and within the single unit, complete defoliation has been confined, so far, to blocks of some 25–30ha. This, at least, is the sum of our 30 years experience of this pest on *P. sylvestris*. It appears, however, that *B. piniaria*, like so many other insects, has a predilection for *P. contorta* but we have very little information of the insect's attack pattern on this pine.

The factors predisposing the crop to outbreak, so long and well documented in central Europe, apply equally well in Britain.

A largish forest of *c.* 25–30 years old, in an area of low rainfall (500–600mm) and on poor sandy soil are classical parameters for periodic mass increase. However, a single exception to this formula must be recorded from a boggy young forest of *P. contorta* in north-east Scotland. Perhaps here the stresses requisite for mass increase were derived from a restricted root development brought about by particularly adverse soil conditions rather than from any lack in water or nutrient supply to the site.

With few important exceptions most of our *P. sylvestris* crops lie in higher rainfall areas and enjoy better soil conditions than are associated with high *B. piniaria* hazard rating. Barbour's analysis of population behaviour in a number of Scottish and English forests[21] has put a little meat on more subjective opinions, and it seems clear from his work that given the data for a period of successive years' population assessments, one can characterise the plainly susceptible forests and those unlikely to experience outbreak. His evidence, moreover, goes some way to suggesting the mechanisms which may or may not come into play to control populations naturally.

Over the comparatively short period of our experience with *B. piniaria* as a pest it has been possible to develop something approaching an integrated pest management strategy for the species. In the short term, imminent outbreak is signalled by routine annual counts of pupae made in each putatively susceptible forest unit. Defoliation, unlike that by *Panolis flammae*, does not kill trees directly but the immediate and inevitable secondary mass attack by the bark beetle *Tomicus piniperda* is lethal. Emergency aerial spraying to prevent defoliation is therefore essential if the crop is to be saved.

There are then a number of alternative strategies available to the manager. If conditions are suitable, he may merely decide gradually to change his tree species to the relatively resistant *P. nigra* var. *maritima* in the course of normal felling and over a period of years, repeating the spraying operation meanwhile as and when populations of *B. piniaria* threaten defoliation and loss of crop. In other circumstances he may find that he can realise a higher potential profitability from the site by additions of nutrients and perhaps also fairly energetic site amelioration in terms of cultivation. For instance, the breaking of pans or indurated layers with powerful machinery may allow the introduction of more demanding species such as *Picea*, *Abies* or a broadleaved species.

Since outbreak in Britain is normally limited to fairly small patches of forest, full exploitation of damaged produce can be planned before degrade takes place. In such a way it may be possible to put forward the longer term plan for a change to more profitable species and, at the same time, to minimise financial loss as well as present and future costs of treatment. Where it is known, therefore, that a change of species is either possible or desirable there may be a case for allowing nature to take its course and defoliation to take place.

Life cycle diagram for the Pine looper moth

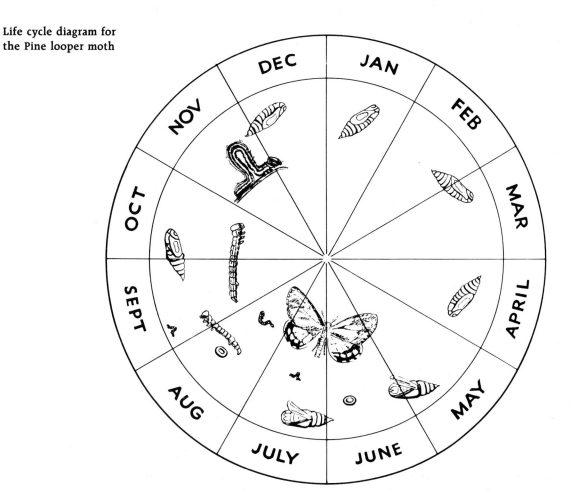

Panolis flammea

History

The Pine beauty moth is a native species feeding on *Pinus sylvestris*, Scots pine. It is very well known as a serious pest of this pine in central Europe over a region, incidentally, which overlaps that prone to attack by the Pine looper moth *Bupalus piniaria*. Population levels in Britain have been recorded over the years as a by-product of the routine surveys of Pine looper pupae. The surveys have included all major crops of Scots pine deemed to be susceptible to damage. Though by no means uncommon, Pine beauty had always remained at low levels until a sudden outbreak occurred in 1976 on young unsurveyed *Pinus contorta* in Sutherland. Attacks spread throughout Caithness and Sutherland in 1977 and by 1978 included an outlier in Moray and another 300 miles to the south in Kirkcudbrightshire. A second outbreak over the northernmost counties started in 1984 and continues up to the time of writing (1986). These outbreaks have necessitated aerial spraying on an unprecedented scale.

Life cycle

Adults – Late March to May
Eggs   – April and early May
Larvae – Early June to late July
Pupae   – From July to the following spring in the litter

Forest importance

There are several features to note in these outbreaks. In the first place there is a curious dearth of parasitoids present; although most species taken in other parts of Britain have been recorded, numbers have been small. Again there is a strong correlation between outbreak and site geology and soil. All northern incidents have occurred on schists and gneisses of the Moine series and the single southerly one on the physically and chemically rather similar Silurian shales. Both are outstandingly low in nutrients and tend to form heavy and poorly drained soils. All affected sites are covered by 'unflushed' climatic blanket peat and the epicentres of outbreaks have been where the conditions are most severe[23].

The insect shows intriguing non-conformity with the mainland European model of its population ecology[81, 118]. The set of critical spring and summer temperature conditions, for instance, which are taken to characterise the susceptible site in central Europe are never attained in N. Scotland. The behaviour, too, is different in detail, e.g. the hatching larvae feed on needles and never the bud, and it is the 4th instar which shifts from new to old needles not the third. There is also some indication that the optimum proportion of components in the pheromone system may be different in the two areas. These are minor details perhaps but they suggest that selection processes have been at work and that we may have an island variant on our hands.

PINE SHOOT MOTH Plate 66 (see also p.81).

Rhyacionia buoliana

History

Pine shoot moth was one of a handful of pests which threatened to be limiting in the early days of pine plantation forestry in the south of Britain. The early incidences of 'posthorns' and double stems caused concern and led to early attempts at introducing parasitoids for the pest's biological control. As crops grew, thinning gradually removed the damaged stems. It appeared soon that early damage had reduced the value of these intermediate yields by only a small margin and crops remaining retained few signs of the early damage.

Life cycle

Adult – End of June to early August
Eggs   – July/August
Larvae – August overwintering to June
Pupae – June/July

Forest importance

It is rather fortunate that this moth is confined to the south of Britain, its extreme northerly distribution as a species being Dumfries. It is another species native to Scots pine, with an outstanding preference for *Pinus contorta*, and in this case *P. muricata*. Damage to the two pines on the few southern heathlands on which they have been tried has usually resulted in heavy repeated attacks upon a high proportion of trees in the crop. The peak of this pattern may be seen on some of the Old Red Sandstone areas in southern Ireland where choice of species is severely limited by site factors and the problem therefore is a serious one. Growth of the pine here is extremely fast but the plentiful resin flow which accompanies this lush performance seems to provide no resistance to invasion of the tree's buds and new shoots.

LARCH BUD MOTH Plate 74 (see also pp.65, 71, 79).

Zeiraphera diniana

History

A species best known in the Alps for its regularly cycling defoliation of *Larix decidua*[20]. It seems that the complete stripping of the trees takes place about every 10 or 11 years. In intermediate years late-flushing of the larch brought about by the damage favours a variant in the population, which prefers spruce or pine as food. This variant is dubbed 'the pine form' and the larvae are grey-green in colour whilst the typical 'larch form' is duller brownish[73]. Intermediates exist. The full story is that the damaged trees gradually recover vigour and synchrony with the larch form which, in turn, leads to a further period of damage. In Britain both forms occur but those intermediate in colour are by far the most common.

It is plain, however, that the insect is on the margin of its distribution as a pest in this country. On one occasion only in the late 1960s (in the English Midlands) has there been defoliation of larch. Similarly there has been only one incidence of serious damage to *P. sitchensis* in N. England in the late 1950s although the species may commonly be found on this spruce. However, once again *Pinus contorta* in northern Britain has proven to be outstandingly susceptible to a species native to *P. sylvestris* (and, of course, *L. decidua*).

Life cycle[73]

Adults – August/September
Eggs   – August/May under bark scales and twigs
Larvae – Late May/early June to mid July in a web
Pupae   – July/August in the nest in pine, in the ground on under larch

Forest importance

The moth cannot, by itself, be considered a major pest in Britain although locally, where soil conditions are particularly adverse, it may cause serious distortions to tree form particularly where attack over successive years occurs. A combination of damage to current year's growth through needle mining by *Z. diniana* and removal of older foliage by the sawfly *Neodiprion sertifer* (see p.133) has caused local tree mortality and justifiable alarm.

A pheromone has demonstrated useful activity, has been synthesised and used in the field. The pheromones of the pine and larch forms are chemically slightly different but both materials appear attractive to British stock.

Cephalcia lariciphila

History

The species was first collected in Britain[136] in 1953 at Alice Holt Forest (Hants) and again in Wytham Wood (Oxon.) in 1954 whilst contemporary surveys failed to record it elsewhere. Complete, annually repeated, defoliations of *Larix kaempferi* and *L.* x *eurolepis*, began in 1972 in mid-Glamorgan, Wales[35]. The sawfly subsequently spread throughout Wales and the greater part of England as far north as Grizedale in Cumbria and was collected in Peebles in 1983. Pest populations peaked in about 1977/78 when over 2000 hectares were reported as defoliated. The Ichneumon parasitoid *Olesicampe monticola*, from a toe-hold in 1976, increased rapidly following the path of outbreak and is reported as the prime cause of a population collapse commencing in 1979 and more or less complete by 1982/83[37].

Life cycle

One generation a year.

Adult   – mid May to mid June

Eggs   – singly on short shoots on underside of needles towards tip

Larvae   – June to mid July, on all needles feeding from a silk tube in spring

Pupae   – Usually at the mineral and organic soil interface without a cocoon; overwintering as a diapausing prepupa, pupating in spring

Forest importance

C. lariciphila has twice before in Europe demonstrated its ability for prodigious increase in the absence of natural enemies. The first of these in Holland lasted some 9 years from 1941–1950[105] and the second in N. Germany for about 3 years from 1948–50[115]. Both of these prolonged outbreaks collapsed through parasites and in both cases they were species other than our own *O. monticola*[37]. It would seem that in these instances, natural controls were slow to reach to man-made plantation forests of *Larix kaempferi*, the Japanese larch, presumably travelling from alpine stock of *C. lariciphila* feeding on *L. europaea*. Once they had arrived, however, they appeared to have established themselves and thenceforth contained the *C. lariciphila* population at low endemic level. There have been no further reports of damage since the first outbreak though in Holland at least specimens of the pest can still be collected. An outbreak in Asian USSR during 1978 is also reported[143].

There seems every reason to hope, therefore, that the final chapter on the sawfly as a pest in Britain will have been written within the next year or so if this is not already the case. Spread of the sawfly is likely to continue but the transplantation of its parasite has proven to be easy and biological control in any new pocket of outbreak should be a matter of routine.

EUROPEAN SPRUCE SAWFLY Plate 35 (see also p.69).

Gilpinia hercyniae

History

The story of this sawfly in Britain has an interesting parallel to that of *Cephalcia lariciphila* (see p.131) in that both were relatively newly introduced exotic pest species and both came under control through natural agencies hitherto unrecorded in Britain. The single outbreaks of the two perhaps represent characteristic passing stages in the early years of afforestation rather than events likely to be repeated many times over in the fashion of established pest species.

G. hercyniae was first recorded in Britain in 1906 and had been taken in 18 counties of England and Wales by 1983[34]. A minor outbreak in Northamptonshire from 1948–50 caused slight defoliation of *Picea omorika*. From 1968 to 1974, however, populations erupted in central Wales and damage to *P. sitchensis* and *P. abies* was widespread and locally serious. In 1971 a powerful baculovirus entered the arena, introduced and spread, it is thought, by birds[78] This, in combination with the outstandingly cold and wet summer of 1974, saw a dramatic collapse of populations.

Life cycle[34]

Adult — May/June (a mainly parthenogenetic species, males being extremely rare)
Eggs — May to mid-July
Larvae — June to September/October
Pupae — September to May

Forest importance

The insect in Wales has a single generation in the year (and it is possible that it even failed to complete this in 1974). In Canada it is known to complete two generations over a wide range and up to three in warmer parts. It is likely therefore that distribution of the species in Britain may be limited by climatic factors[35]. The arrival in the country of the virus and the known presence of one or two species of insect parasites suggests that some balance may now have been struck between the pest and its natural enemies.

It may be worth recording that the particular area over which the outbreak occurred has been recognised as an area deficient in phosphorus for good spruce growth. The applications of ground mineral phosphate made to the crops since the outbreaks will undoubtedly affect their general health and growth and with it perhaps their resistance to increase of the sawfly.

Neodiprion sertifer and Diprion pini

History

There are seven diprionid sawflies recorded in Britain, one of these is very common, one fairly, and another occasionally so – the rest are rare. *N. sertifer* and *D. pini* were well known in pine plantings on heathland in the south during the 1920s and 30s. *D. simile* was also quite often found in company with *D. pini*. These sawflies give a quite dramatic performance being large, coloured and, feeding in large colonies, cause severe, if often only localised, damage. Gloves were therefore issued and hand destruction of colonies followed! Further experience taught that outbreaks were normally shortlived and recovery good. It seemed that disease could be relied on to appear in the case of *N. sertifer*, the cause of which was later to be identified as a highly specific, active and therefore useful nuclear polyhedrosis virus[79]. The virus is now in service on a commercial scale as a biological control agent. *D. pini*, on the other hand, proved to be consistently dealt with by a company of equally reliable parasitoids. The course of outbreaks in both species seemed to follow onset to peak and collapse in about 3 years.

Life cycle[4]

N. sertifer

One generation a year.

Adult   – September/October
Eggs   – Overwintering, single or in broken rows in needle edges
Larvae – Late May to July
Pupae   – July/September in strong ovoid cocoon in soil; occasionally overwintering individuals spin to foliage[137]

D. pini

Two generations a year.

Adult   – May/June and July/August
Eggs   – In rows in needle edge covered over with foam-like, hard roofing
Larvae – End of June/July and August/September
Pupae   – July/August in soil or foliage and September in soil

Forest importance

Both species are pests of young forest[9] although *D. pini* is recognised as an occasional important pest of older pines in parts of mainland Europe. *N. sertifer*, however, is certainly more noticeable and perhaps more significant in younger, i.e. pre-thicket, crops. At the peak of outbreak *N. sertifer* can strip the trees of all old foliage leaving only tufts of current year's needles. *D. pini* eats the current years needles first and then proceeds down the branch. Typically the species is found on parts of the crowns only and quite often on the lower branches on crop margins of young pole stage pine.

Modern interest in the pine sawflies is centred on *N. sertifer* damage to *Pinus contorta* in Scotland. This pine appears to be very attractive to the species as indeed it does to so many insects native to *Pinus sylvestris*. Recovery of *P. contorta* from damage is assured despite its serious appearance at the peak of outbreak. However, there is a set-back in growth and establishment under the frequently adverse site conditions and competing vegetation in parts of north Scotland. It has been calculated that this set-back sums to about 3 or 4 years delay in harvesting.

There is also a rather special case where defoliation of older foliage by *N. sertifer* is followed by damage to new growth by the Grey larch tortrix moth *Zeiraphera diniana* (see also p.130). This combination has caused death of individual plants as well as crown distortions and scant recovery throughout the afflicted crop.

Elatobium abietinum

History

Green spruce aphid must be classed together with its host, *Picea*, as an exotic, although one of long standing. The aphid was quick to show itself in the early days of the wide scale reafforestation of the country which followed the first world war. The urgency then was to create a living reserve bank of softwood timber. The long-fibred spruce was the obvious choice of genus to supply it and the fast-growing *P. sitchensis* was the species to bring about the objective most speedily. Ample evidence was to hand from N. Europe, from our own arboreta and from specimen trees to confirm the choice and so the spruce was planted over a very wide range of site conditions.

Out of the first decade or so of planting soon emerged one of those empirical 'rules' typical of growers the world over – the '40″ (1000mm) of rainfall and over for Sitka' rule! The rule represented the sum of experience of the practical man in his particular environment. It also summed the capabilities of the aphid to survive in all but the coldest of British winters, to continue to multiply in mild ones, and to take full advantage of trees periodically drought stressed through being planted on heavy soils restrictive of root development or on those too freely draining to retain moisture. Records show that serious defoliation occurs over a large part of Britain every 3–5 years, whilst 10 or more years is typical, for instance, in the Low Countries[53]

Life cycle

The aphid's pattern of development is fairly predictable in the south but shows some variation with increase of latitude and altitude. A sexual and egg stage have been found infrequently (whilst the egg is the normal overwintering stage in more continental climates, it is the exception in Britain). *E. abietinum* is therefore a parthenogenetic species in Britain.

Wingless adults and nymphs may be found throughout the year on spruce needles but are most likely to be seen from about August through to the beginning of the following June.

Short-lived winged adults begin to appear usually in May and, in the south, by the middle of June have produced minute larvae which appear to enter a summer diapause, remaining in small numbers without further development for some 6 weeks or so. Growth then starts again and numbers increase.

Forest importance

Carter has shown that very considerable losses in tree increment can result from severe defoliation[53]. Such losses in growth and defoliation itself mean different things to different growers. The nurseryman is concerned with producing young, fully foliated plants of good colour up to a specified height as quickly as possible. The Christmas tree grower[57] (see also pp.137–8) also requires high quality foliage but may need even to restrict growth to get a desirable, fairly short jointed, 'toy-town' conical shape. Both these growers may require pesticides to achieve desired results. The forester has a prime interest in producing wood. He will have chosen the species he plants to suit the site and soil and seldom, if ever, would find it justifiable, on economic grounds alone, to boost productivity with pesticides.

The commercial forester has to rely on his initial planting procedures of species choice and ground preparation being such that the mean growth of the crop will provide an economically acceptable performance over a period of time. He expects there to be fluctuations in annual growth brought about by variation in all the factors of the environment, including insect feeding. He must seek his answers to the control of pests such as *E. abietinum*, which reduce growth but seldom kill, in terms of integrated, or what he prefers to term silvicultural controls. This may take the form of some change in cultural practice; or in the choice of seed source or provenance to benefit the tree's defences against the insect; or he may seek a solution through the selection or breeding of trees with known resistance[59]. In general, sap-suckers such as aphids are insidious in their mode of action and their control demands an intimate knowledge of the relationship between the host tree and the feeding insects.

Regeneration Pests of Conifers

PINE WEEVIL Plate 39 (see also p.59).

Hylobius abietis

History

There can be few if any forest insects about which more has, over the centuries, been written[76]. It is the only one of all the European forest pests against which prophylactic treatment is routine and essential if the regeneration of conifer crops is to be assured[104]. The root system of felled or dead coniferous trees and to some extent the underside of the lying stem is the weevil's normal breeding niche. Its distribution is throughout Europe and much of northern Asia.

Life cycle

From 1 to 2 years in Britain and as much as 3+ years in northern parts of Scandinavia.

Adult	– Long-lived and present all year round; feeding upon and ring-barking of young trees tends to peak in early spring and again in July/throughout August
Eggs	– Larvae and pupae may be found at all times of the year.

Forest importance

H. abietis feeds as an adult on the green bark of young trees of all conifers frequently killing them. It may, however, turn its attention to young wood in the crowns of surrounding older trees and frequently strips bramble (*Rubus fruticosa*) or young broadleaved plants. The maintenance of a high endemic population of the weevil is an inevitable result of production forestry. The species breeds in conifer stumps left after thinning and clear felling as well as the root systems of natural casualties. It is therefore a built in accompaniment to normal forest practice.

Unfortunately vagaries in dispersal lead to difficulties in predicting precise pattern. Flight of the adult does appear to be most common in the young newly emerged beetle and in conditions of higher temperature during sunny periods. However, the species has a reputation for 'walking to work', rather than flying and thus the presence of stumps within an area under regeneration is assumed to constitute the greatest hazard. The assumption will certainly prove to be justified in a high proportion of cases and particularly where a forest enterprise is under commercial management for sustained annual yield of felled produce. However, it is not uncommon for a 'one-off' felling followed by an unprotected replant to escape the weevil but such a gamble is not to be recommended.

Experimental plantings on bare soil are reported to be less prone to attack than those made on more weedy sites[62] and it may certainly be true that, given the choice, weevils may favour one condition rather than another. It is doubtful, however, whether hungry individuals of such an adaptable species would be inhibited to any useful degree if no choice existed.

BLACK PINE AND SPRUCE BEETLES[104] Plate 38 (see also pp.75 & 83).

Hylastes spp.

History

These beetles have proved to be rather more aggressive under British conditions than in many other parts of Europe. They have, over the years and on occasion, been held to have played the major part in planting losses, particularly of pine, and are currently giving some trouble to containerised plants.

Life cycle

Adults – Peaking in March/May and August/September; present all year round
Eggs – April/May and August/September and later; present all year round
Larvae – May/June and August/September and later; present all year round
Pupae – June and September and later

Overwinter as an adult or larvae.

Forest importance

Much that has already been said about *H. abietis* applies also to *Hylastes* spp. They share the same breeding sites in the root system of felled trees though *Hylastes* appears to choose a somewhat longer-felled stump than does the weevil, preferring it to be some 6 months or so after cutting. The beetle is typically most important in forests which have reached the sustained production stage in which regular annual coupes are a feature. Continuous fellings in contiguous blocks of pine provide optimum conditions for the species to increase.

Damage occurs at the root collar region and is often confined to the stem and root below soil level. A dead plant therefore shows little or no visible sign for the cause of death. The natural urge to pull it up to examine its root will leave all evidence in the ground; such removal must be done carefully when the frass, damaged tissue and sometimes the beetle will provide clear evidence as to where guilt should be layed.

CLAY-COLOURED WEEVIL Plate 52 (see p.59).

Otiorhynchus singularis

History

This is perhaps not strictly a pest of regeneration as it is of plantings in grassy sites generally. Early plantings on *Molinia caerulea* (Purple moor grass), particularly in South Wales, suffered badly from ring-barking by adults of this weevil in the early days of afforestation.

Life cycle

Adult – April/October
Eggs – throughout the year below ground
Larvae – throughout the year below ground
Pupae – throughout the year below ground

Forest importance

The larvae of this weevil are found feeding on grasses and fine roots of both trees and herbs. The adult is flightless and tends therefore seldom to stray to sites where a grassy vegetation is absent. It feeds on a very wide range of woody plants and is often found in association with another weevil *Strophosomus melanogrammus*, Plate 67 (see also p.59) which feeds in a similar way but usually on finer twigs.

Damage where *Larix* is being regenerated, replaced or underplanted is common and broadleaves may also be attacked. Of the conifers *Tsuga heterophyla* appears to be favoured.

Christmas Tree Pests

Plates 2, 31, 32, 50, 62 (see also pp.67, 69, 71).

The Christmas tree in Britain is traditionally a Norway Spruce, *Picea abies*, though in other countries it is often another conifer. Some of these reach the market as by-products of normal forest practice being 'tops' from fellings or planned early removals from crops planted at higher than normal density. Such trees are subject to forest conditions and we can assume that a tree's selection or rejection for sale will be dependent on whether it has or has not reached a required standard. Such opportunities for selection are not, however, presented to the specialist grower of crops raised specifically for the Christmas tree market. His cultures are intensively managed; and economic considerations, and therefore his philosophy of pest control, are closer to that of the farmer than the forester. In commercial practice such crops are normally raised successively, a practice which can intensify problems. The grower's object is to produce a high yield of plants with maximum foliage retention and good shape acceptable to the top of the market.

Unfortunately *Picea abies* is not really a very good ecological fit to the drier parts of Britain. This leads the grower not only into a number of tricks of the trade in growing technique but also into a need to pay careful attention to pest control. Prophylactic applications of insecticides against particularly persistent species are commonly used and the possibility of such practices leading to outbreak is always present (in analogous fashion to similar troubles in fruit orchards, for instance).

The following are the commonest species to cause damage in intensive culture:

CONIFER SPINNING MITE (see also p.67).

Oligonychus ununguis

This mite is commonly found on a variety of conifers and particularly spruces grown in dry, hot conditions. The mite is barely visible to the naked eye in any stage but the tell-tale silk which it spins wherever it goes is conspicuous in spring and summer when numbers are large, forming a haphazard network of fine silk threads on the needles and shoots. The mite overwinters as an egg. These hatch in May or June as pale opalescent, yellowish-green immature mites which move to the needles and suck the sap. There are several over-lapping summer generations and all stages may then be found. The needles turn firstly a dirty-greyish-yellow and later bronze.

Serious damage does seem to be characteristic of certain sites and infestation tends there to repeat itself in successive years. Spraying, however, should be consequent upon the finding of massed eggs on shoots. Routine, prophylactic treatments are not to be advised on ground of the known ability of mites to develop strains resistant to acaricides in a matter of a few generations. Treatments should be started at egg hatch in May and repeated fortnightly sprays may become necessary.

PINEAPPLE GALL WOOLLY APHID (see also p.71).

Adelges abietis

This is the only Adelgid species to confine its attentions to spruce species alone. It can, therefore, build up a high population on a single tree or crop over a period of years. Galls formed on lower, less vigorous shoots, tend to terminate the shoot whilst upper more vigorous shoots tend to grow on past the gall but at an angle from normal growth. Both galls and distortions are unsightly and can render stock unsaleable. Preventive action is necessary where this insect is known to be a pest and needs to be taken before gall initiation. Contact insecticides applied on mild days between November and the end of February have been found effective.

GREEN SPRUCE APHID (see also pp.67 & 134).

Elatobium abietinum

A small green aphid which feeds on the underside of all needles, except those of the newly formed current year's growth, causing them to yellow and fall off. The aphid spends the winter as potentially active adults and nymphs. Both stages are quick into action at the onset of mild temperatures and can be found feeding whenever winter conditions allow. Typically in southern Britain damage starts in March/April, reaches a peak in May, and abruptly ceases (with the development of a winged generation) at the beginning of June. Less obvious damage may occur in Sept./Oct. when aphid numbers can increase particularly in mild seasons. The pattern becomes less sharp with increased latitude and/or altitude. In the Border country, between England and Scotland, for instance, and occasionally in parts of Ireland, very serious defoliation may take place in late autumn and early winter, and the aphid seems generally to be fine-tuned to its host plant as a provider of food.

Whilst mild weather is a prerequisite for increase, cold and frost constitute the dominant natural control to outbreak[51]. The grower then has strong weather signals to examine his crops for potentially dangerous increase of this aphid. When regular trouble is experienced treatment is best carried out commencing late Aug./Sept. but should be dependent on insects found. The aphid is not difficult to control with any one of a number of aphicides and it is suggested that treatment should follow insect numbers rather than be routine.

BROWN SPRUCE SHOOT APHID (see also p.71).

Cinara pilicornis

The colonies of brown and/or grey aphids are to be found feeding on new shoots in May and June and have usually disappeared by July. Occasionally the needles discolour some-what to yellow and feeding may put a slight snake into the leading shoot but on the whole the tree shows little sign of infestation. However, the aphid produces great quantities of honeydew and trees may become blackened with the sooty moulds which grow upon it and render it unattractive and unsaleable. A single early treatment as soon as colonies are spotted will normally be sufficient to cure the trouble.

SPRUCE BELL MOTH (see also p.69).

Epinotia tedella

This can be a severe pest but will normally occur only where Christmas trees are grown, say, as a catch crop, in woodland conditions and where there are older spruce trees. The moth is common on the lower branches of such trees and does little damage but it can cause severe loss in cosmetic value to Christmas trees. The larvae mine the needles, spinning them together and to the shoots in bundles during autumn and winter. The needles turn brown and later fall through the action of wind and rain, leaving bare patches on the shoot. Early damage becomes obvious when the first needles begin to turn colour. Remedial action should be taken in the period August to October if degrade is to be avoided.

GREGARIOUS SPRUCE SAWFLY (see also p.69).

Pristiphora abietina

Again where Christmas trees are grown near to older spruce trees this sawfly may cause loss of current year's needles and sometimes die-back of the shoot. The larvae, which are of similar colour to the needle, may be found feeding on them in colonies during May and June. The feeding time is therefore short and intervention must be prompt upon first sighting of damage if degrade is to be avoided.

References

1. ADAMS, P.H.W. and ENTWISTLE, P.F. (1981). *An annotated bibliography of Gilpinia hercyniae (Hartig), European spruce sawfly.* Commonwealth Forestry Institute, Occasional Paper 11.

2. ALDHOUS, J.R. and BROWN, R.M. (1959). Control of cutworms in forest nurseries. *Forestry* 32 (2), 155–156.

3. ANON. (1952). *Pissodes weevils.* Forestry Commission Leaflet 29. HMSO, London.

4. ANON. (1955). *Pine sawflies.* Forestry Commission Leaflet 35. HMSO, London.

5. ANON. (c.1979). *The Lackey moth (Malacosoma neustria).* Advisory Leaflet 7, Portsmouth City Council.

6. ANON. (1981). *Web-forming caterpillars.* Ministry of Agriculture, Leaflet 40.

7. ASKEW, R.R. (1962). The distribution of galls of *Neuroterus* (Hym.: Cynipidae) on oak. *Journal of Animal Ecology* 31, 439–455.

8. ATKINS, P.M., O'CALLAGHAN, D.P. and KIRBY, S.G. (1981). *Scolytus laevis* (Chapuis) (Col.: Scolytidae) new to Britain. *Entomologist's Gazette* 32 (4), 280.

9. AUSTARA, Ø. (1987). Defoliation by the Pine sawfly *Neodiprion sertifer* – effect on growth and economic consequences. In, *Population biology and control of the Pine beauty moth*, eds. S.R. Leather, J.T. Stoakley and H.F. Evans. Forestry Commission Bulletin 67. HMSO, London.

10. BAKER, J.M. (1963). Ambrosia beetles and their fungi with particular reference to *Platypus cylindrus* (F.). *Symposium of the Society for General Microbiology* 13, 323–324.

11. BAKER, J.M. (1965). Aspects of the life history of the Ambrosia beetle *Platypus cylindrus* (F.). *Proceedings of the 12th International Congress of Entomology* 695–696.

12. BAKKE, A. (1958). Mass attack of *Brachonyx pineti* Payk. (Col.: Curculionidae) on pine forests in Norway. *Meddelelser, Norsk Skogforsøksvesen* 15, 124–142.

13. BAKKE, A. (1963). Studies on the Spruce cone insects *Laspeyresia strobilella* (L.) (Lep.: Tortricidae), *Kaltenbachiola strobi* (Winn.) (Dip.: Itonidae) and their parasites (Hym.) in Norway. Biology, distribution and diapause. *Report of the Norwegian Forest Research Institute* 67, **XIX**.

14. BAKKE, A. (1968). Field and laboratory studies on sex ratio in *Ips acuminatus* (Col.: Scolytidae) in Norway. *Canadian Entomologist* 100 (6), 640–648.

15. BAKKE, A. (1968). Ecological studies on bark beetles (Col.: Scolytidae) associated with Scots pine (*Pinus sylvestris*) in Norway with particular reference to the influence of temperature. *Meddelelser, Norsk Skogforsøksvesen* 21, 441–602.

16. BAKKE, A. (1975). Aggregation pheromone in the bark beetle *Ips duplicatus* (Sahlberg). *Norwegian Journal of Entomology* 22, 67–69.

17. BAKKE, A., AUSTARÅ, Ø. and PETTERSEN, H. (1977). Seasonal flight activity and attack pattern of *Ips typographus* in Norway under epidemic conditions. *Meddelelser, Norsk Institut for Skogførskning* 33 (6), 256–258.

18. BAKKE, A., SAETHER, T. and KVAMME, T. (1983). Mass trapping of the Spruce bark beetle *Ips typographus*. Pheromone and trap technology. *Meddelelser, Norsk Institut for Skogførskning* 38 (3), 2–35.

19. BALE, J.S. (1981). Seasonal distribution and migratory behaviour of the Beech leaf mining weevil *Rhynchaenus fagi* L. *Ecological Entomology* 6, 109–118.

20. BALTENSWEILER, W., BENZ, G., BOVEY, P. and DELUCCHI, V. (1977). Dynamics of Larch bud moth (*Zeiraphera*

diniana (Gn.)) populations. *Annual Review of Entomology* **22**, 79–100.

21. BARBOUR, D.A. (1985). Patterns of population fluctuation in the Pine looper moth *Bupalus piniaria* L. in Britain. In, *Site characteristics and population dynamics of Lepidopteran and Hymenopteran forest pests*, eds. D. Bevan and J.T. Stoakley. Forestry Commission Research and Development Paper 135, 8–20. Forestry Commission, Edinburgh.

22. BARNES, H.F. (1951). *Gall midges of economic importance. V. Gall midges of trees.* Crosby Lockwood, London.

23. BARNET, D.W. (1987). Pine beauty moth outbreaks – associations with soil type, host nutrient status and tree vigour. In, *Population biology and control of the Pine beauty moth*, eds. S.R. Leather, J.T. Stoakley and H.F. Evans. Forestry Commission Bulletin 67. HMSO, London.

24. BARSON, G. and CARTER, C.I. (1972). A species of Phylloxeridae, *Moritiziella corticallis* (Kalt.) (Homoptera) new to Britain, and a key to British oak feeding Phylloxeridae. *The Entomologist* **105**, 130–134.

25. BEJER, B. (1985). *Dendroctonus micans* in Denmark. In, *Biological control of bark beetles (Dendroctonus micans)*. Proceedings of an EEC symposium, Brussels, 1984.

26. BETTS, M.M. (1958). Notes on the life history of *Ernamonia conicolana* (Heyl.), (Lep.: Eucosmidae). *Entomologist's Monthly Magazine* **94**, 134–137.

27. BEVAN, D. (1962). The Ambrosia beetle or Pinhole borer *Trypodendron lineatum* O1. *Scottish Forestry* **16**, 94–99.

28. BEVAN, D. (1965). *Bourletiella signata* (Nicol), (Collembola) – a pest of conifer seedlings. *Proceedings of the 12th International Congress of Entomology*, London, 1964.

29. BEVAN, D. (1971). Notes on *Pissodes validirostris* Gyll. and *P. pini* L. (Col.: Curculionidae). *Entomologist's Monthly Magazine* **107**, 90.

30. BEVAN, D. (1972). Control of forest insects: there is a porpoise close behind us. In, *Biology in pest control*, eds. D. Price Jones and M.E. Solomon. 13th Symposium of the British Ecological Society.

31. BEVAN, D. and BROWN, R.M. (1978). *Pine looper moth*. Forestry Commission Forest Record 119. HMSO, London.

32. BEVAN, D. and KING, C.J. (1983). *Dendroctonus micans* Kug. – a new pest of spruce in UK. *Commonwealth Forestry Review* **62** (1), 41–51.

33. BEVAN, D. (1984). Coping with infestation. *Quarterly Journal of Forestry* **38**, 36–40.

34. BILLANY, D.J. (1978). *Gilpinia hercyniae – a pest of spruce*. Forestry Commission Forest Record 117. HMSO, London.

35. BILLANY, D.J. and BROWN, R.M. (1980). The Web-spinning sawfly *Cephalcia lariciphila* (Wachtl) (Hym.: Pamphiliidae) – a new pest of larch in England and Wales. *Forestry* **53** (1), 71–80.

36. BILLANY, D.J., CARTER, C.I., WINTER, T.G. and FIELDING, N.J. (1983). The effects of climate and parasites on *Gilpinia hercyniae* (Hartig) (Hym.: Diprionidae) in Britain. *Entomologist's Monthly Magazine* **119**, 117–120.

37. BILLANY, D.J., WINTER, T.G. and GOULD, I.D. (1985). *Olesicampe monticola* (Hedwig) (Hym.: Ichneumonidae) redescribed together with notes on its biology as a parasite of *Cephalcia lariciphila* (Wachtl) (Hym.: Pamphiliidae). *Bulletin of Entomological Research* **75**, 267–274.

38. BLACKMAN, R.L. (1964). *Aphids*. Ginn & Co. Ltd., London and Aylesbury.

39. BLETCHLY, J.D. and WHITE, M.G. (1962). Significance and control of attack by the Ambrosia beetle *Trypodendron lineatum* (Oliv.) (Col.: Scolytidae) in Argyllshire forests. *Forestry* **35**, 139–163.

40. BLETCHLY, J.D. (1967). *Insects and marine borer damage to timber and woodwork*. Ministry of Technology, Forest Products Research.

41. BORDEN, J.H. (1982). Aggregation pheromones. In, *Bark beetles in North American conifers*, 74–140, J.B. Mitton and K.B. Sturgeon.

42. BRADLEY, J.D., TREMEWAN, W.G. and SMITH, A. (1973). *British tortricoid moths – Cochylidae and Tortricidae: Tortricinae*. Ray Society.

43. BRADLEY, J.D. (1977). *British tortricoid moths – Tortricidae: Olethreutinae.* Ray Society.

44. BRIGHT, D.E. (1976). *The bark beetles of Canada and Alaska – Coleoptera: Scolytoidea.* Canadian Department of Agriculture Publication 1576.

45. BROWNE, F.G. (1968). *Pests and diseases of forest plantation trees. An annotated list of the principal species occuring in the British Commonwealth.* Clarendon Press, Oxford.

46. BURDEKIN, D.A. (Ed.) (1983). *Research on Dutch elm disease in Europe.* Forestry Commission Bulletin 60. HMSO, London.

47. BUSE, A. (1977). The importance of birds in the dispersal of nuclear polyhedrosis virus of European spruce sawfly *Gilpinia hercyniae* (Hym.: Diprionidae) in mid-Wales. *Entomologia Experimentalis et Applicata* **22**, 191–199.

48. CARTER, C.I. (1956). Massing of *Tetranychus tiliarum* (Hermann) (Acarina: Tetranychidae) on the limbs of lime trees. *Entomologist's Monthly Magazine* **92**, 73–74.

49. CARTER, C.I. (1969). Three species of Adelgids (Homoptera: Adelgidae) new to Britain. *Entomologist's Monthly Magazine* **105**, 167–168.

50. CARTER, C.I. (1971). *Conifer wooly aphids (Adelgidae) in Britain.* Forestry Commission Bulletin 42. HMSO, London.

51. CARTER, C.I. (1972). *Winter temperatures and survival of the Green spruce aphid.* Forestry Commission Forest Record 84. HMSO, London.

52. CARTER, C.I. (1975). *Towards integrated control of tree aphids.* Forestry Commission Forest Record 104. HMSO, London.

53. CARTER, C.I. (1977). *Impact of Green spruce aphid on growth.* Forestry Commission Research and Development Paper 116. Forestry Commission, Edinburgh.

54. CARTER, C.I. and COLE, J. (1977). Flight regulation in the Green spruce aphid (*Elatobium abietinum*). *Annals of Applied Biology* **86**, 137–151.

55. CARTER, C.I. and MASLEN, N.R. (1982). *Conifer lachnids.* Forestry Commission Bulletin 58. HMSO, London.

56. CARTER, C.I. (1982). Susceptibility of *Tilia* species to the aphid *Eucallipterus tiliae. Proceedings of the 5th International Symposium on Insect–Plant Relationships*, Wageningen, 1982.

57. CARTER, C.I. and GIBBS, J.N. (1984). Pests and diseases of forest crops. In, *Pest and disease control handbook*, eds. N. Scopes and M. Ledieu, ch. 15, 575–591.

58. CARTER, C.I. (1983). Some new aphid arrivals in Britain's forests. *Proceedings and Transactions of the British Entomological and Natural History Society* **16**, 81–87.

59. CARTER, C.I. and NICHOLS, J.F.A. (1985). Some resistance features of trees that influence the establishment and development of aphid colonies. *Zeitschrift für angewandte Entomologie* **99**, 64–67.

60. CARTER, C.I. and NICHOLS, J.F.A. (1985). Host plant susceptibility and choice by conifer aphids. In, *Site characteristics and population dynamics of Lepidopteran and Hymenopteran forest pests*, eds. D. Bevan and J.T. Stoakley. Forestry Commission Research and Development Paper 135, 94–100. Forestry Commission, Edinburgh.

61. CHARARAS, C. (1962). Scolytides des conifères. *Encyclopédie Entomologique* **38**.

62. CHRISTIANSEN, E. and BAKKE, A. (1971). Feeding activity of the Pine weevil *Hylobius abietis* (Col.: Curculionidae) during a hot period. *Norsk Entomologisk Tidsskrift* **18**, 110–118.

63. CHRISTIANSEN, E. and HORNTVELDT, R. (1983). Combined *Ips/Ceratocystis* attack on Norway spruce and defensive mechanisms of the trees. *Zeitschrift für angewandte Entomologie* **96**, 110–118.

64. CHRISTIANSEN, E. (1985). *Ips/Ceratocystis* infection of Norway spruce: what is a deadly dosage? *Zeitschrift für angewandte Entomologie* **99**, 6–11.

65. CHRYSTAL, R.N. (1937). *Insects of the British woodlands.* Warne.

66. COOKE, R.C. and RAYNER, A.D.M. (1984). *Ecology of spermotrophic fungi*. Longman. (Ch. 9, Wood).

67. CROOKE, M. (1953). Some notes on *Anoplonyx destructor*. *Bulletin of Entomological Research* **44**, 77–81.

68. CROOKE, M. and BEVAN, D. (1957). Notes on the first occurrence of *Ips cembrae* (Heer) (Col.: Scolytidae). *Forestry* **30**, 21–28.

69. CROOKE, M. (1959). Insecticidal control of the Pine looper in Great Britain. I. Aerial spraying. *Forestry* **32**, 166–196.

70. DARLINGTON, A. (1968). *The pocket encyclopaedia of plant galls*. Blandford.

71. DARLINGTON, A. (1974). The galls on oak. In, *The British oak – its history and natural history*, eds. M.G. Morris and F.H. Perring. BSBI, Faringdon.

72. DAVIES, J.M. and KING, C.J. (1977). *Pine shoot beetles*. Forestry Commission Leaflet 3. HMSO, London.

73. DAY, K. (1984). Phenology, polymorphism and insect-plant relationships of the bud moth *Zeiraphera diniana* (Genee) (Lep.: Tortricidae) on alternative conifer hosts in Britain. *Bulletin of Entomological Research* **74**, 47–64.

74. DOOM, D. (1966). The biology, damage and control of the poplar and willow borer *Cryptorrhynchus lapathi*. *Netherlands Journal of Plant Pathology* **72**, 233–240.

75. DUFFY, E.A.J. (1953). *A monograph of the immature stages of British and imported timber beetles (Cerambycidae)*. British Museum (Natural History).

76. EIDMANN, H.H. (1971). *Selected literature on Hylobius abietis L. and related species*. (Bibliography). Research Notes 9, Department of Zoology, Royal College of Forestry, Stockholm.

77. ENTWISTLE, P.F. (1971). Possibilities of control of a British outbreak of Spruce sawfly by a virus disease. *Proceedings of the 6th British Insecticide and Fungicide Conference* 475–479.

78. ENTWISTLE, P.F., ADAMS, P.H.W. and EVANS, H.F. (1977). The epizootology of a NPV in European spruce sawfly (*G. hercyniae*): the status of birds as dispersal agents of the virus during the larval season. *Journal of Invertebrate Pathology* **29**, 354–360.

79. ENTWISTLE, P.F., EVANS, H.F., HARRAP, K.A. and ROBERTSON, J.S. (1985). Control of European pine sawfly *Neodiprion sertifer* (Geoffr.) with its nuclear polyhedrosis virus in Scotland. In, *Site characteristics and population dynamics of Lepidopteran and Hymenopteran forest pests*, eds. D. Bevan and J.T. Stoakley, Forestry Commission Research and Development Paper 135, 36–46. Forestry Commission, Edinburgh.

80. ESCHERICH, K. (1923). *Die forstinsekten mitteleuropas* **2**. Paul Parey, Berlin.

81. ESCHERICH, K. (1931). *Die forstinsekten mitteleuropas*, **3**. Paul Parey, Berlin.

82. EVANS, G.O., SHEALS, J.G. and MacFARLANE, D. (1961). *The terrestrial acari of the British Isles* **1**, 114. British Museum (Natural History).

83. FAIRHURST, C.P. and KING, C.J. (1983). The effect of climatic factors on the dispersal of elm bark beetles. In, *Research on Dutch elm disease in Britain*, ed. D.A. Burdekin, Forestry Commission Bulletin 60, 40–46. HMSO, London.

84. FAO (1958). *Poplars in forestry and land use*. Food and Agriculture Organization of the United Nations, Forestry and Forest Products Studies 12.

85. FRANKE-GROSSMANN, H. (1962). Ungewohnlich Knospenschaden an Sitkafichten. *Proceedings of the 12th International Congress of Entomology* **2**, 189–191.

86. GIBB, J.A. (1958). Predation by tits and squirrels on the Eucosmid *Ernarmonia conicolana* (Heyl.). *Journal of Animal Ecology* **27**, 375–396.

87. GIBB, J.A. (1966). Tit predation and the abundance of *Ernarmonia conicolana* (Heyl.) on Weeting Heath, Norfolk. *Journal of Animal Ecology* **35**, 43–53.

88. GIBBS, J.N., BURDEKIN, D.A. and BRASIER, C.M. (1977). *Dutch elm disease*. Forestry Commission Forest Record 115. HMSO, London.

89. GIBBS, J.N. (1984). *Oak wilt*. Forestry Commission Forest Record 126. HMSO, London.

90. GREGOIRE, J-C. (1985). *Dendroctonus micans* – the evolution of a brood system. In, *Biological control of bark beetles*, eds. J-C. Gregoire and J.M. Pasteels. Proceedings of a seminar organised by the Commission of the European Communities and the Université Libre, Brussels.

91. GREIG, B.J.W. (1981). *Decay fungi in conifers*. Forestry Commission Leaflet 79. Forestry Commission, Edinburgh.

92. GRIJPMA, P. (1985). *Dendroctonus micans* (Kug.) in the Netherlands – the situation today. In, *Biological control of bark beetles*, eds. J-C. Gregoire and J.M. Pasteels. Proceedings of a seminar organised by the Commission of the European Communities and the Université Libre, Brussels.

93. HAYES, A.J. and SHIPP, V.M. (1983). Distribution of the Green spruce needle miner *Epinotia nanana* (Treitschke) (Lep.: Tortricidae) within and between trees at Redesdale, Northumberland. *Forestry* **56**(2), 195–205.

94. HEATH, J. and EMMET, A.M. (1985). *The moths and butterflies of Great Britain and Ireland* 2. British Museum (Natural History).

95. HERING, E.M. (1951). *Biology of leaf miners*. Junk, The Netherlands.

96. HUSSEY, N.W., READ, W.P. and HESLING, J.S. (1969). *The pests of protected cultivation*. Edward Arnold.

97. HUTCHINSON, H.P. and KEARNS, H.G.H. (1931). The control of *Galerucella lineola* – a major pest of willows. *Report of the Agricultural and Horticultural Research Station, Bristol, 1930*, 108–111.

98. HUTCHINSON, H.P. and KEARNS, H.G.H. (1931). The control of *Phyllodecta vitellinae* L. (Chrysomelidae) – a major pest of willows. *Report of the Agricultural and Horticultural Research Station, Bristol, 1930*, 112–126.

99. JUKES, M.R. (1984). *The Knopper gall*. Arboriculture Research Note 55/84/ENT. DoE Arboricultural Advisory and Information Service, Forestry Commission, Edinburgh.

100. KIRBY, S.G. and FAIRHURST, C.P. (1983). The ecology of elm bark beetles in northern Britain. In, *Research on Dutch elm disease in Europe*, ed. D.A. Burdekin, Forestry Commission Bulletin 60, 29–39. HMSO, London.

101. KOLOMIETS, M.G., STADNITSKII, G.V. and VORONTZOV, A.I. (1972). *The European pine sawfly*. (Translation). Amerind Publishing Co. Pty. Ltd.

102. KYLONIEUS, A.F. and BEROZA, M. (1982). *Insect suppression with controlled release pheromone systems*. CRC Press, Florida.

103. LEKANDER, B., BEJER-PETERSEN, B., KANGAS, E. and BAKKE, A. (1977). The distribution of bark beetles in the Nordic countries. *Acta Entomologica Fennica* **32**, 1–36.

104. LOW, A.J. (Ed.) (1985). *Guide to upland restocking practice*. Forestry Commission Leaflet 84. HMSO, London.

105. LUITJES, J. and MINDERMAN, G. (1959). Die spinselbladwesp vande lariks. *Nederlands Bosbouw Tijdschrift* **31**, 245–253.

106. MacDOUGALL, R.S. (1923). The Holly leaf miner. *Transactions of the Highland Agricultural Society, Scotland* **35**, 125–126.

107. McMULLEN, L.N. (1976). *Spruce weevil damage – ecological basis and hazard rating for Vancouver Island*. Canadian Forestry Service.

108. OSSIANNILSON, F. (1981). The Auchenorrhyncha (Homoptera) of Fennoscandia and Denmark. *Fauna Entomologica Scandinavica* **7** (2), 223–593.

109. PEACE, T.R. (1952). *Poplars*. Forestry Commission Bulletin 19. HMSO, London.

110. PILON, J.G. (1965). Bionomics of the Spruce budworm *Zeiraphera ratzeburgiana* (Ratz.) (Lep.: Oleuthreutidae). *Phytoprotection* **46** (1), 5–13. Canadian Department of Forestry.

111. RAFFA, K.F. and BERRYMAN, A.A. (1982). Physiological differences between Lodgepole pine resistant and susceptible to the Mountain pine beetle and associated micro-organisms. *Environmental Entomology* **11** (2), 486–492.

112. REDFERN, D.B. and STOAKLEY, J.T. Personal communication: (*Ips cembrae* and associated fungus).

113. REDFERN, D.B. Personal communication: (*Ips acuminatus* associated with *Trichosporium tingens*).

114. REDFERN, M. (1975). The life history and morphology of the early stages of the Yew gall midge *Taxomyia taxi* (Inchbald) (Dip.: Cecidomyidae). *Journal of Natural History* **9**, 513–533.

115. RÖHRIG, E. (1953). Die Lärchengespinstblattwespe *Cephalcia alpina* Klug. Untersuchungen bei einer Massenvermehrung in Schleswig-Holstein. *Zeitschrift für angewandte Entomologie* **35**, 207–245.

116. SCHWENKE, W. (1972). *Die Forstschädlinge Europas*. **1**. *Wurmer, Schnecken, Spinnentiere, Taussendfüssler und hemimetabol Einsekten*. Paul Parey, Hamburg and Berlin.

117. SCHWENKE, W. (1974). *Die Forstschädlinge Europas*. **2**. *Käfer*. Paul Parey, Hamburg and Berlin.

118. SCHWENKE, W. (1978). *Die Forstschädlinge Europas*. **3**. *Schmetterlinge*. Paul Parey, Hamburg and Berlin.

119. SCHWENKE, W. (1982). *Die Forstschädlinge Europas*. **4**. *Hautflügler und Zweiflugler*. Paul Parey, Hamburg and Berlin.

120. SCOTT, T.M. (1972). *The Pine shoot moth and related species*. Forestry Commission Forest Record 83. HMSO, London.

121. SCOTT, T.M. and KING, C.J. (1974). *The Large pine weevil and Black pine beetles*. Forestry Commission Leaflet 58. HMSO, London.

122. SCOTT, T.M. (1975). *Experiments with insecticides for the control of Dutch elm disease*. Forestry Commission Forest Record 105. HMSO, London.

123. SMITH, B.D. and STOTT, K.G. (1964). The life history of the Willow weevil *Cryptorrhynchus lapathi* L. *Annals of Applied Biology* **54**, 141–151.

124. SMITH, S.G. and SUGDEN, B.A. (1969). Host trees and breeding sites of native North America *Pissodes* bark weevils, with a note on synonymy. *Annals of the Entomological Society of America* **62**, 146–148.

125. SPEIGHT, M.R. (1983). Tree pests: Longhorn beetles (family Cerambycidae). *Arboricultural Journal* **7**, 13–16.

126. SPEIGHT, M.R. and NICOL, M. (1984). Horse chestnut scale – a new urban menace? *New Scientist* **101** (1404), 40–42.

127. STERLING, P.H. (1985). *The Brown-tail moth*. Arboriculture Research Note 57/85/ENT. DoE Arboricultural Advisory and Information Service, Forestry Commission, Edinburgh.

128. STOAKLEY, J.T. (1966). The period of oviposition by the Douglas fir seed wasp. *Forestry Commission Report on Forest Research 1965*, 185–189. HMSO, London.

129. STOAKLEY, J.T. (1973). Laboratory and field tests of insecticides against Douglas fir seed wasp (*Megastigmus spermotrophus* Wachtl). *Plant Pathology* **22**, 79–87.

130. STOAKLEY, J.T. (1977). A severe outbreak of the Pine beauty moth on Lodgepole pine in Sutherland. *Scottish Forestry* **31** (2), 113–125.

131. STOAKLEY, J.T., BAKKE, A., RENWICK, J.A.A. and VITE, J.P. (1977). The aggregation pheromone system of the Larch bark beetle *Ips cembrae* Heer. *Zeitschrift für angewandte Entomologie* **86**, 174–177.

132. STOAKLEY, J.T. (1979). *Pine beauty moth*. Forestry Commission Forest Record 120. HMSO, London.

133. STOAKLEY, J.T. (in preparation). *Ips cembrae*. Forestry Commission.

134. STROYAN, H.L.G. (1964). Notes on some British species of *Pemphigus* Hartig (Homoptera: Aphidoidea) forming galls on poplar, with the description of a new species. *Proceedings of the Royal Entomological Society of London* (B) **33**, 92–100.

135. STROYAN, H.L.G. (1975). The life cycle and generic position of *Aphis tremulae* L. 1761 (Aphidoidea: Pemphiginae), with a description of the viviparous morphs and a discussion of spruce root aphids in the British Isles. *Biological Journal of the Linnean Society* **7**, 45–72.

136. STYLES, J. (1959). Notes on the collection of the adults and the web-spinning larvae of *Cephalcia alpina* Klug. (Hym.: Pamphiliidae). *Entomologist's Monthly Magazine* **95**, 152–153.

137. STYLES, J.H. (1960). Observations on the spinning of cocoons by larvae of the sawfly *Neodiprion sertifer* (Geoff.) (Hym.: Diprionidae). *Entomologist's Monthly Magazine* **95**, 178–179.

138. TENOW, O. (1972). The outbreaks of *Oporinia autumnata* Bkh. and *Operophtera* spp. (Lep.: Geometridae) in the Scandinavian mountain chain and northern Finland 1862–1968. *Zoologiska Bidrag* Sup. 2, 12–23. Uppsala.

139. TRAGÅRDTH, I. (1939). *Sveriges Skogsinsekter*. Gaber, Stockholm.

140. VARLEY, G.C. and GRADWELL, G.R. (1962). The effect of partial defoliation by caterpillars on the timber production of oak trees in England. *Proceedings of the 11th International Congress of Entomology* **2**, 211–214.

141. VARLEY, G.C. and GRADWELL, G.R. (1973). *Insect population ecology*, 112–134. Blackwell.

142. VIEDMA, M.G. de (1972). A note on a character to separate *Pissodes notatus* and *P. validirostris* Gyll. (Col.: Curculionidae). *Entomologist's Monthly Magazine* **108**, 79.

143. VERZHUTSKII, B.N., PLESHANOV, A.S., POTAPOV, V. and EPORA, V.I. (1979). An outbreak of the Larch web-spinning sawfly *Cephalcia lariciphila* in the North Baikal Region. *Report of the Institute of Geography of Siberia and the Far East* 72–74. Siberian Institute of Plant Physiology and Biochemistry, Irkutsk.

144. WAINHOUSE, D. (1979). Dispersal of the Beech scale (*Cryptococcus fagi* Baer.) in relation to the development of Beech bark disease. *Mitteilungen der Entomologische Gesellschaft, Basel* **52**, 181–183. Bulletin of the Swiss Entomological Society.

145. WAINHOUSE, D. and HOWELL, R.S. (1983). Intraspecific variation in Beech scale populations and in susceptibility of their host *Fagus sylvatica*. *Ecological Entomology* **8**, 351–359.

146. WALKER, C. (1973). Interception of the North American elm bark beetle (*Hylurgopinus rufipes* Eichh.) imported from Canada into Britain in logs of Rock elm (*Ulmus thomasii* Sarg.). *Plant Pathology* **22** (3), 147.

147. WATERS, W.E. (1985). The Pine bark beetle ecosystem – a pest management challenge. In, *Integrated pest management in Pine bark beetle ecosystems*, eds. W.E. Waters, R.W. Stark and D.L. Wood. John Wiley, Chichester and New York.

148. WATT, A.S. (1957). Beech regeneration in Lodge Wood, Hampden, Bucks. *Quarterly Journal of Forestry* **51**, 73–74.

149. WHITNEY, H.S. (1982). Relationships between bark beetles and symbiotic organisms. In, *Bark beetles in North American conifers* 183–212, J.B. Mitton and K.B. Sturgeon, University of Texas.

150. WINTER, T.G. (1978). *A seed wasp affecting the Wild service tree (Sorbus torminalis)*. Arboriculture Research Note 3/78/ENT. DoE Arboricultural Advisory and Information Service, Forestry Commission, Edinburgh.

151. WINTER, T.G. (1979). Observations on the biology and some larval parasites of *Rhyacionia duplana logaea* Durrant (Lep.: Tortricidae) in Scotland. *Entomologist's Gazette* **30** (4), 257–265.

152. WINTER, T.G. (1981). The larvae of *Rhyacionia duplana logaea* Durrant (Lep.: Tortricidae) described and compared with *R. duplana duplana* (Hubner) and *R. simulata* (Heinrich). *Entomologist's Gazette* **32**, 233–242.

153. WINTER, T.G. (1984). Wind assisted dispersal of *Tortrix viridana* (L.) (Lep.: Tortricidae) from West Sussex. *Entomologist's Monthly Magazine* **120**, 245–251.

154. WINTER, T.G. (1985). Is *Ips typographus* a British insect? *Entomologist's Gazette* **36**, 153–160.

155. WOOD, S.L. (1963). A revision of the bark beetle genus *Dendroctonus* Erichson (Col.: Scolytidae). *Great Basin Naturalist* **23**, 1–117.

Index

(Numerals in bold type indicate pages on which illustrations are to be found.)

Printed in the United Kingdom for Her Majesty's Stationery Office by A.P.B. Process Print Ltd.   Dd 739223   C60   3/87